✦ LOOPS *&* LATTES HIKING SERIES ✦

Copyright © 2016 Nicola Ross

Third printing October 2021

**Halton Hikes: Loops & Lattes** - 37 Loop Routes
Published by Woodrising Consulting Inc.
Alton, Ontario L7K 0C4

For ordering information visit
**www.loopsandlattes.ca**

✦ ✦ ✦

To read Nicola's travel and hiking blog, visit
**nicolaross.ca**

Library and Archives Canada Cataloguing in Publication

Ross, Nicola, author
Halton hikes : loops & lattes : 37 loop routes / Nicola Ross.

ISBN 978-0-9940302-1-4 (paperback)

1. Hiking--Ontario--Halton--Guidebooks.  2. Trails--Ontario--
Halton--Guidebooks.  3. Halton (Ont.)--Guidebooks.  I. Title.

GV199.44.C22H346 2016   796.5109713'533   C2016-906061-6

Cover painting by Julia Veenstra
Edited by Lori-Ann Livngston
Design by Gillian Stead
All photographs and maps by Nicola Ross unless otherwise noted.

DISCLAIMER
The information in the maps and text in this book have been well researched by
ourselves, other organizations and volunteers, and tested by a team of beta testers.
We cannot be held liable for any inaccuracies that may be present within the maps or text.
Remember:
• Hazards exist along the trails.
• You are responsible for your own safety.
• Be properly prepared.

**Note: All maps are approximations and not meant
to precisely delineate private from public lands.**

Printed in Canada by Friesens – Printed on FSC certified paper

ABOUT THE COVER
*The Red Barns*

**Julia Veenstra** is a Canadian artist
whose paintings reflect the joy
she sees in the world. Her choice
of acrylic paint allows her to use
expressive strokes in vibrant colours.
Julia says, "I hope to reflect in my
work moments that cause a stirring
in a person's heart." She paints in her
Hamilton studio on images that
are recognized across Canada.

Visit **juliaveenstra.com**
to view Julia's paintings.

MIX
Paper from
responsible sources
FSC® C016245
FSC
www.fsc.org

## + 37 LOOP ROUTES +

## Nicola Ross

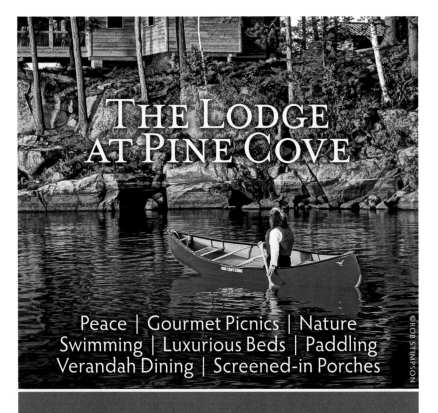

# THE LODGE AT PINE COVE

Peace | Gourmet Picnics | Nature
Swimming | Luxurious Beds | Paddling
Verandah Dining | Screened-in Porches

©ROB STIMPSON

The Lodge at Pine Cove on the historic French River is closer than you think.

"To think that just 3½ hours from our front door we could enjoy such spectacular scenery, completely devoid of others, is amazing." The Carnegies, Caledon, Ontario

"It is so rare to find such a wonderful combination of natural beauty, world-class paddling and exceptional hospitality." The Sandishoes, Chicago, Illinois

## Enjoy Nicola's hiking trails at The Lodge at Pine Cove.

*Discover the French River*

info@frenchriver.com **frenchriver.com** 705-898-2500

# Generous Sponsors

*Halton Hikes: Loops & Lattes* is more of a community project than a book. Myriad businesses, organizations and hikers have been part of its creation. A few of them went a step further and actually sponsored a hike or two. I encourage you to frequent their businesses.

THE LODGE AT PINE COVE
Discover the French River

Caledon Hills Cycling & Nordic Centre

HAMILTON HALTON BRANT
FIND YOUR WAY TO THE HEART OF ONTARIO

GREEN BELT
Possibility grows here

est. 1977
HEATHERLEA
FARM SHOPPE

CHELTENHAM General Store
Since 1887

Conservation Halton

SPIRIT TREE
ESTATE CIDERY

Wild Birds Unlimited
Nature Shop

LOCALLY OWNED AND ENJOYED
Lakeshore Coffee House
2007 LAKESHORE RD BURLINGTON

the Tin Roof Café

TRIBECA
COFFEE CO. EST. 2016

FLYING MONKEY BIKE SHOP
& COFFEE BAR

Jill Johnson
SALES REPRESENTATIVE
Outstanding Service, Outstanding Results!
905.877.8262
www.jilljohnson.ca
ROYAL LEPAGE 100 YEARS
Meadowtowne Realty, Brokerage
Independently Owned and Operated

PEARTREE
Bed & Breakfast

EST. 2015
COPPER KETTLE CAFÉ

Dr. Elizabeth Dimovski
Home of the FREE Custom Mouth Guard
For all of our sports-playing patients!
WE PROTECT YOUR SMILE!
905-458-6620

Credit Valley Conservation
inspired by nature

Copper Kettle PUB

EXPEDICIONES SIERRA NORTE
PUEBLOS MANCOMUNADOS
OAXACA

# Contents

Acknowledgments 11

Introduction 13

How to Use This Guide

 Consider / Refer to the Guide 15

 What You Need to Know about Hiking in Halton 16

Trailhead Locations Map 17

Loop Routes by Distance Chart 18

## The Loops

 Loop 1 Apple Cidery Loop (Cheltenham) 23

 Loop 2 Authors' Way Loop (Georgetown) 27

 Loop 3 Bear Den Loop (Acton/Rockwood) * 33

 Loop 4 Burlington Beach Route 37

 Loop 5 Burlington Waterfront/Nicola's Folly Loop 41

 Loop 6 Crawford Lake Loop (Campbellville) 45

 Loop 7 Crawford Lake to Rattlesnake Point Route * 51

  (Campbellville)

 Loop 8 Credit Valley Footpath "Best-Of" Loop (Glen Williams) 57

 Loop 9 Donovan Bailey/Bronte Village Loop 61

 Loop 10 Dufferin Gap Route (Speyside/Campbellville) * 67

 Loop 11 Erin Village Loop 73

 Loop 12 Erin Village/Stanley Park Loop 77

 Loop 13 Felker's & Albion Falls Loop (Hamilton) 83

 Loop 14 Glen Abbey Loop (Oakville) 87

 Loop 15 Glen Williams Village Loop 91

= NEW HIKE  * These loops have shorter and longer options.

## The Loops *continued*

| | | |
|---|---|---|
| Loop **16** | Great Esker Loop (Terra Cotta/Glen Williams) | 95 |
| Loop **17** | Guelph Radial Line Linear Route (Rockwood/Acton) * | 99 |
| Loop **18** | Halton Forest Multiple Options Loop (Milton) * | 105 |
| Loop **19** | Hendrie Valley Loop (Burlington) * | 111 |
| Loop **20** | Hilton Falls Loop (Campbellville) * | 117 |
| Loop **21** | "Hole in the Wall" Figure Eight Loop (Limehouse) * | 121 |
| Loop **22** | Hungry Hollow Loop (Georgetown) | 127 |
| Loop **23** | Joshua's Creek South Loop (Oakville) | 131 |
| Loop **24** | Kelso Cliffs Loop (Campbellville) | 137 |
| Loop **25** | Limehouse Combo Loop | 141 |
| Loop **26** | MapleCross Nature Reserve Loop (Campbellville/Kilbride) | 147 |
| Loop **27** | Mt. Nemo/Sarah Harmer Tribute Loop (Lowville) * | 151 |

PHOTO BY ANNE CROWE

| Loop 28 | Mountsberg Pioneer & Lookout Combo Loop * (Campbellville) | 155 |
| Loop 29 | Rattray Marsh Loop (Mississauga) | 161 |
| Loop 30 | Rockwood Pothole Loop | 165 |
| Loop 31 | Scotsdale Farm/Duff Pit Loop * (Georgetown/Glen Williams) | 171 |
| Loop 32 | Sixteen Mile Creek Loop (Oakville) | 175 |
| Loop 33 | Speyside North Route (Milton/Speyside) | 179 |
| Loop 34 | Terra Cotta Footpath Loop | 183 |
| Loop 35 | Terra Cotta Wolf Lake Loop | 187 |
| Loop 36 | Walking Fern/Silver Creek Loop (Glen Williams) | 191 |
| Loop 37 | Waterdown/Offa's Dyke Loop | 195 |
| Tribute to Shirley White | | 207 |
| The Loopy Ladies | | 208 |

= NEW HIKE                    * These loops have shorter and longer options.

Winifred & Dave Hunsburger ▲

Heather Kendall ▲    Hiker Mike Davis ▼

Margaret Shier ▲    David & Mary Tinsley ▼

Linda Pim ▲    Ute Lippold ▼

*Our enthusiastic beta testers make sure that when I write "right," I mean "right."*

Michael Treuman ▲    Richard Olley ▼

Some of the Wednesday Walkers ▲

Anne Crowe & Ian Davis ▲

*The 2021 Wednesday Walkers include:* Paula Basciano, Carol Blackmere, Shirley Edgerton, Cheri Gregory, Mary Margaret Greyerbiehl, Bett Leverette, Diane Madden, Dorothy Mazeau, Tory McMahon, Susan Millar, Julia Sarazin, Louise Stewart, Ann Waddon, Shirley White and Cathy Whitcombe.

# Acknowledgments

When I set out to revise the 37 hikes in this guide, it seemed a mighty task. It looked nearly impossible when I sprained my right knee. The injury was serious enough that it took more than three, largely hike-less, months to heal. Fortunately for me, enthusiastic hikers and the pandemic combined to make this rewrite not just possible, but a wonderful team effort.

With a new brace, a handful of anti-inflammatories and a bag of ice precariously balanced on my affected knee, I called the beta testers who had helped out before. It was midway through the lockdown of early 2021 and, it turned out, many of them were at loose ends. They jumped at the prospect of having a reason to get out onto the hiking trails, practically falling over each other to give me an update on one or two or eight or nine different hikes. Sometimes they returned to a trail a couple of times to be absolutely sure they were correct. Many of them contributed photos and added stories about cats on leashes and sightings of remarkable birds or prized flowers.

As a result, I ended up with 37 shiny, spiffed up hikes, several of them brand spanking new to submit to my ever-patient editor, Lori-Ann Livingston. Then they were off to Gillian Stead to be laid out in book form. This is the seventh time Gill has been my partner on these hiking guides. Our business relationship has turned into a much-valued friendship.

Once again, a big thanks to the hiking associations, conservation authorities, government agencies, landowners, volunteers, cities, towns and villages that created and now maintain the rich collection of trails that make this guide possible.

# Introduction

*"My Loops & Lattes hiking guide is the best lockdown gift ever!"*

Sheena Costello, Feb. 11, 2021

T his completely updated edition of *Halton Hikes: Loops & Lattes* is a pandemic baby. When I wrote the first version in 2016, no one could have guessed that hiking would become a lifeline for so many people. Dozens of hikers have written to me with stories of how local trails helped them get through the shutdowns, shut-ins and general lack of access to other activities. Melodie Bronsema explained, "I love the idea of a weekend hike and thought working through your hiking guide could be a positive goal to help fight the COVID blues." Stephen Hogkins related a wonderful story about how his 15-year-old, device-addicted daughter graduated from short walks to wanting to hike the entire Bruce Trail.

With the pandemic hopefully coming to an end or at least a steadier state, I hope that people continue to hit the trails, getting to know the trees, flowers, hills, cliffs, valleys and the critters who call Halton home.

This updated version of *Halton Hikes: Loops & Lattes* includes five entirely new hikes, as well as several that have been much improved. The changes reflect updated signage, trail closures, new restaurants and, sadly, closed ones. Where appropriate, I've added a reference to the related Bruce Trail map and replaced some of the photos with better ones. What hasn't changed is that this guide takes advantage of the cliffs at Kelso, Mt. Nemo and Rattlesnake Point. It explores the rocky trails in the near wilderness of the Silver Creek and Terra Cotta areas, and the well-crafted boardwalks through the Royal Botanical Gardens and along the former Guelph Radial Line. It continues to alert readers to the wonderful restaurants and cafés that have struggled through incredibly tough closures, re-openings and re-closures.

*This trail demands to be followed.*

I was once again wowed by the hiking in Burlington and Oakville. I added a brand-new route in the Glen Abbey area. Another of the new routes takes you to the 40-metre-long Dufferin Gap. It's a devastating break in the otherwise uninterrupted 725k-long, 450-million-year-old Niagara Escarpment. Also new is a loop that runs north from Speyside near Milton/Acton as well as a wonderful hike near Terra Cotta. The 24.1k Guelph Radial Line Linear Route has a few Covid closures, so I've described three separate, shorter in-and-out routes that make it more approachable. I replaced the Yaremko-Ridley Park/Lovely Creek Loop with a shorter double figure-8 route through the MapleCross Nature Reserve because of a trail closure in Kilbride.

> *"Single trees are extraordinary; trees in number more extraordinary still. To walk in a wood is to find fault with Socrates's declaration that 'Trees and open country cannot teach me anything, whereas men in town do.'"*
>
> from: *The Old Ways: A Journey on Foot*, by Robert Macfarlane

What hasn't changed, however, is the robust selection of trails in Halton with the region's rich cultural and natural history. Also unaltered are the positive effects of hiking on people such as Ellen Marshall. She writes, "You inspired me at 72 to have my first ever year of winter hiking, which has been a godsend this pandemic year! Just wonderful."

I believe I speak for all hikers when I thank the conservation authorities, parks personnel, private property owners, trail associations and their volunteers who keep our trails open and safe, especially during these pandemic months. And perhaps most important of all, our thanks for having access to the hiking routes situated on the traditional territory of the Mississaugas of the Credit, part of the Anishinaabe Nation. We hope this guidebook will play some small part in raising awareness about the beauty of nature and the need to respect our natural lands.

Nicola Ross, October 2021

# How to Use This Guide

## Consider

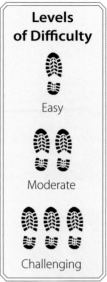

- ✦ *What length of hike do you want?* While the hikes are ordered alphabetically, the Loop Routes by Distance chart on page 18 lists them by length, from shortest (about 1 hour) to longest (up to about 8 hours).

- ✦ *How difficult a hike do you want?* The chart tells you whether a hike is Easy (mostly flat with good footing), Moderate (some hills and/or rocky and uneven terrain) or Challenging (lots of hills and/or rocky and uneven terrain).

- ✦ *What type of hike would you prefer?* Do you want to walk along a forested trail on the Niagara Escarpment or meander through more open terrain? You can stay away from roads altogether or follow a route that finds nature in a town or a beach in a city. The Overview and map for each hike gives you a sense of what it will be like.

- ✦ *Do you want to carry a picnic or stop along the way at a restaurant, café or general store?* Nicola's Insider Info for each hike tells you if there is somewhere to stop en route for food and/or drinks.

## Refer to the Guide

- ✦ Look at the Loop Routes by Distance chart on page 18 and find the hikes that are your desired length and level of difficulty.

- ✦ Read Nicola's Insider Info to determine which of the suitable routes offers your preferred way of keeping your feet and stomach happy.

- ✦ Read through the Overview and Directions for the routes that are right for you.

- ✦ Select your route.

- ✦ Refer to the Trailhead Locations map on page 17. It shows you where to park and begin (and end) your selected route. GPS coordinates for each trailhead are included in the Loop Routes By Distance chart on page 18, but do not rely entirely on them. Make sure the GPS coordinates are taking you to the spot indicated on the map.

# The Blazes

**Turn Right**

**Turn Left**

**Straight On**

**Trail Ends**

Figure 1

## What You Need to Know about Hiking in Halton

✦ All the routes in this guide follow established trails or roads that are accessible to the public. If you want to keep having access to these routes, respect the land and stay on the trail.

✦ Maintaining access to public lands often requires diligent effort by citizens. Get to know what lands around you are public and ensure they are protected for public use and/or for environmental stewardship.

✦ Where routes follow roads, they are almost always quiet back roads with minimal traffic. Occasionally, it was necessary to include a short walk on a busy road to close the loop.

✦ Understand how to "read" the blazes used by the Bruce Trail and the Guelph Hiking Trail Club. See Figure 1 at left.

✦ Support the agencies and organizations that build and maintain the trails. Buy a membership to the Bruce Trail Conservancy, the Guelph Hiking Trail Club, Conservation Halton, Credit Valley Conservation, Grand River Conservation Authority and/or the Royal Botanical Gardens.

✦ Keep your dog on a leash and under control.

✦ Stoop and scoop if your dog deposits on a trail, sidewalk or someone's lawn. If trail signage says "No Dogs," obey it.

✦ Wear comfortable clothes, a hat and running or hiking shoes. The trails can be slippery so take care.

✦ Don't litter.

✦ Learn to recognize poison ivy.

✦ Park in the designated areas described in this guide.

✦ Carry insect repellent, sunscreen, a bit of cash and water.

✦ When walking on a road without much of a shoulder, cross over to the right side if going up a blind hill or around the inside of a corner. It's safer.

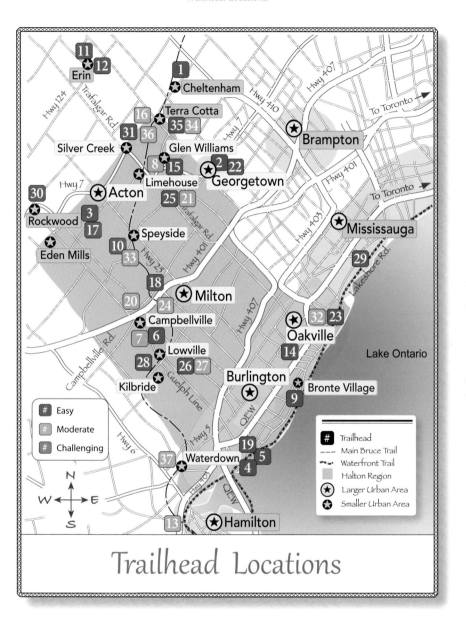

# Trailhead Locations

"The path, no matter where it takes you,
leads you back to yourself."

ELIZABETH GANONG

# Loop Routes — BY DISTANCE

| Loop # | Route Name | Closest Town/Village | Start/End Point | Trailhead GPS | Length (k) | Hiking Time (hrs) | * Level of Difficulty | Page # |
|---|---|---|---|---|---|---|---|---|
| 21 | "Hole in the Wall" Figure Eight Loop (short) | Limehouse | Village of Limehouse | N43° 38.297' W79° 58.742' | 3.6 | 1 to 1.5 | 2 | 121 |
| 19 | Hendrie Valley Loop (short) | Burlington | Hendrie Valley parking lot on Plains Rd. & Botanical Dr. | N43° 17.534' W79° 53.177' | 3.9 | 1 to 1.5 | 1 | 111 |
| 31 | Scotsdale Farm/ Duff Pit Loop (short) | Georgetown/ Glen Williams | Scotsdale Farm from Trafalgar Rd. | N43° 41.245' W79° 59.443' | 4.2 | 1 to 1.5 | 1 | 171 |
| 15 | Glen Williams Village Loop | Glen Williams | 22nd Sdrd. and 10th Line | N43° 41.100' W79° 55.598' | 4.6 | 1 to 1.5 | 1 | 91 |
| 35 | Terra Cotta Wolf Lake Loop | Terra Cotta | Terra Cotta Conservation Area | N43° 43.393' W79° 57.435' | 5 | 1.25 to 1.75 | 1 | 187 |
| 18 | Halton Forest Multiple Options Loop (short) | Milton | Southerly parking lot for the Britton Tract on 6th Line | N43° 32.200' W79° 58.711' | 5 | 1.25 to 1.75 | 1 | 105 |
| 26 | Maple Cross Nature Reserve Loop | Campbellville/ Kilbride | Blind Line & Britannia Rd. | N43° 25.033' W79° 54.670' | 5 | 1.25 to 1.75 | 1 | 147 |
| 30 | Rockwood Pothole Loop | Rockwood | Rockwood Conservation Area | N43° 36.693' W80° 08.902' | 5.1 | 1.5 to 2 | 1 | 165 |
| 5 | Burlington Waterfront/ Nicola's Folly Loop | Burlington | Burloak Regional Waterfront Park | N43° 22.147' W79° 43.665' | 5.3 | 1.5 to 2 | 1 | 41 |
| 27 | Mt. Nemo/ Sarah Harmer Tribute Loop (short) | Lowville | Mt. Nemo Conservation Area | N43° 25.025' W79° 52.917' | 5.3 | 1.5 to 2 | 2 | 151 |
| 3 | Bear Den Loop (short) | Acton/ Rockwood | 5th Line, near Hwy. 7 | N43° 36.201' W80° 05.794' | 5.5 | 1.5 to 2 | 1 | 33 |
| 4 | Burlington Beach Route | Burlington | Lakeshore Rd. and Brant St. | N43° 19.458' W79° 47.770' | 5.6 | 1.5 to 2 | 1 | 37 |
| 2 | Authors' Way Loop | Georgetown | Edith St. parking lot | N43° 38.893' W79° 55.677' | 5.9 | 1.5 to 2 | 1 | 27 |
| 20 | Hilton Falls Loop (short) | Campbellville | Hilton Falls Conservation Area | N43° 30.341' W79° 57.704' | 6.5 | 1.5 to 2.5 | 2 | 117 |
| 23 | Joshua's Creek South Loop | Oakville | Maplegrove Arena at Elmhurst Ave. & Devon Rd. | N43° 28.771' W79° 38.637' | 6.5 | 1.5 to 2.5 | 1 | 131 |
| 28 | Mountsberg Pioneer & Lookout Combo Loop (short) | Campbellville | Mountsberg Conservation Area | N43° 27.597' W80° 01.823' | 6.5 | 1.5 to 2.5 | 1 | 155 |
| 14 | Glen Abbey Loop | Oakville | Glen Abbey Community Centre | N43° 26.104' W79° 44.290' | 6.7 | 1.5 to 2.5 | 1 | 87 |
| 32 | Sixteen Mile Creek Loop | Oakville | Sixteen Hollow Park, Upper Middle Rd. W & Dorval Dr. | N43° 27.134' W79° 44.104' | 7 | 1.5 to 2.5 | 2 | 175 |

**\* LEVELS OF DIFFICULTY:   1 Easy  •  2 Moderate  •  3 Challenging**

# Loop Routes — BY DISTANCE

| Loop # | Route Name | Closest Town/Village | Start/End Point | Trailhead GPS | Length (k) | Hiking Time (hrs) | * Level of Difficulty | Page # |
|---|---|---|---|---|---|---|---|---|
| 6 | Crawford Lake Loop | Campbellville | Crawford Lake Conservation Area | N43° 28.191′ W79° 57.071′ | 7.2 | 1.75 to 2.5 | 1 | 45 |
| 19 | Hendrie Valley Loop (long) | Burlington | Hendrie Valley parking lot on Plains Rd. & Botanical Dr. | N43° 17.534′ W79° 53.177′ | 7.2 | 1.75 to 2.5 | 1 | 111 |
| 21 | "Hole in the Wall" Figure Eight Loop (long) | Limehouse | Village of Limehouse | N43° 38.250′ W79° 58.780′ | 7.2 | 1.75 to 2.5 | 2 | 121 |
| 3 | Bear Den Loop (long) | Acton/ Rockwood | 5th Line, near Hwy. 7 | N43° 36.201′ W80° 05.794′ | 7.5 | 1.75 to 2.5 | 1 | 33 |
| 11 | Erin Village Loop | Erin | Elora Cataract Trailway parking lot | N43° 46.741′ W80° 04.393′ | 7.8 | 2 to 2.5 | 1 | 73 |
| 22 | Hungry Hollow Loop | Georgetown | On Miller Dr., between Lookout Ct. & View Point Cir. | N43° 38.024′ W79° 53.617′ | 7.8 | 2 to 2.5 | 1 | 127 |
| 33 | Speyside North Route | Milton/ Speyside | 15th Sdrd. & Hwy. 25 | N43° 34.984′ W79°58.340′ | 7.8 | 2 to 2.5 | 2 | 179 |
| 9 | Donovan Bailey/ Bronte Village Loop | Oakville | Bronte Athletic Park | N43° 24.052′ W79° 42.404′ | 8.4 | 2 to 3 | 1 | 61 |
| 16 | Great Esker Loop | Terra Cotta/ Glen Williams | Fallbrook Tr. & 27th Sdrd. | N43° 41.528′ W79° 58.021′ | 8.4 | 2 to 3 | 2 | 95 |
| 24 | Kelso Cliffs Loop | Campbellville | Kelso Conservation Area | N43° 30.258′ W79° 56.782′ | 8.7 | 2 to 3 | 2 | 137 |
| 29 | Rattray Marsh Loop | Mississauga | Jack Darling Park | N43° 31.798′ W79° 36.512′ | 8.8 | 2 to 3 | 2 | 161 |
| 36 | Walking Fern/ Silver Creek Loop | Terra Cotta/ Glen Williams | 10th Line, north of 27th Sdrd. | N43° 42.572′ W79° 57.775′ | 8.9 | 2.25 to 3 | 2 | 191 |
| 10 | Dufferin Gap Route (short) | Milton/Acton | St. Helena Rd. | N43° 34.251′ W79° 57.779′ | 9 | 2.25 to 3 | 3 | 67 |
| 17 | Guelph Radial Line Linear Route (short) | Acton | 6th Line Nassagaweya & Pineridge Dr. | N43° 36.493′ W80° 04.727′ | 9 | 2.25 to 3 | 2 | 99 |
| 18 | Halton Forest Multiple Options Loop (long) | Milton | Southerly parking lot for the Britton Tract on 6th Line | N43° 32.200′ W79° 58.711′ | 9 | 2.25 to 3 | 1 | 105 |
| 12 | Erin Village/ Stanley Park Loop | Erin | Elora Cataract Trailway parking lot | N43° 46.741′ W80° 04.393′ | 9.5 | 2.5 to 3.5 | 1 | 77 |
| 13 | Felker's & Albion Falls Loop | Hamilton | Upper King's Forest Park | N43° 12.304′ W79° 49.150′ | 10 | 2.5 to 3.5 | 2 | 83 |
| 20 | Hilton Falls Loop (long) | Campbellville | Hilton Falls Conservation Area | N43° 30.341′ W79° 57.704′ | 10.8 | 2.5 to 3.5 | 2 | 117 |
| 31 | Scotsdale Farm/ Duff Pit Loop (long) | Georgetown/ Glen Williams | Scotsdale Farm from Trafalgar Rd. | N43° 41.245′ W79° 59.443′ | 11.2 | 2.5 to 3.75 | 1 | 171 |

**\* LEVELS OF DIFFICULTY:   1 Easy  •  2 Moderate  •  3 Challenging**

# Loop Routes — BY DISTANCE

| Loop # | Route Name | Closest Town/Village | Start/End Point | Trailhead GPS | Length (k) | Hiking Time (hrs) | * Level of Difficulty | Page # |
|---|---|---|---|---|---|---|---|---|
| 25 | Limehouse Combo Loop | Limehouse | Bruce Tr. parking lot on Regional Rd. 43/ Sdrd. 22 | N43° 37.548′ W79° 59.449′ | 11.5 | 3 to 4 | 1 | 141 |
| 34 | Terra Cotta Footpath Loop | Terra Cotta | Winston Churchill Blvd. north of Terra Cotta | W43° 43.617′ W79° 57.530′ | 12 | 3 to 4 | 2 | 183 |
| 27 | Mt. Nemo/ Sarah Harmer Tribute Loop (long) | Lowville | Blind Line & Britannia Rd. | N43° 25.033′ W79° 54.670′ | 12.4 | 3 to 4 | 2 | 151 |
| 1 | Apple Cidery Loop | Cheltenham | Caledon Trailway parking lot on Creditview Rd. | N43° 46.267′ W79° 55.744′ | 12.5 | 3 to 4 | 2 | 23 |
| 7 | Crawford Lake to Rattlesnake Point Route (short) | Campbellville | Crawford Lake Conservation Area | N43° 28.191′ W79° 57.071′ | 12.9 | 3 to 4.5 | 2 | 51 |
| 10 | Dufferin Gap Route (long) | Milton/Acton | BTC's Pear Tree parking lot on 15th Sdrd & Hwy. 25 | N43° 34.678′ W79° 58.619′ | 14 | 3.5 to 5 | 3 | 67 |
| 28 | Mountsberg Pioneer & Lookout Combo Loop (long) | Campbellville | Mountsberg Conservation Area | N43° 27.597′ W80° 01.823′ | 14 | 3.5 to 5 | 1 | 155 |
| 18 | Halton Forest Multiple Options Loop (longest) | Milton | Southerly parking lot for the Britton Tract on 6th Line | N43° 32.200′ W79° 58.711′ | 14.4 | 3.5 to 5 | 1 | 105 |
| 8 | Credit Valley Footpath "Best-Of" Loop | Glen Williams | 22nd Sdrd. and the 10th Line | N43° 39.736′ W79° 54.506′ | 14.6 | 3.5 to 5 | 2 | 57 |
| 37 | Waterdown/ Offa's Dyke Loop | Waterdown | Smokey Hollow parking lot on Waterdown Rd. | N43° 19.854′ W79° 53.220′ | 14.6 | 3.5 to 5 | 2 | 195 |
| 7 | Crawford Lake to Rattlesnake Point Route (long) | Campbellville | Crawford Lake Conservation Area | N43° 28.191′ W79° 57.071′ | 19 | 4.5 to 6.5 | 2 | 51 |
| 17 | Guelph Radial Line Linear Route (long) | Rockwood/ Acton | Start 2nd Line, south of 30th Sdrd./ End Limehouse | N43° 34.229′ W80° 07.507′ | 24.1 | 6 to 8 | 3 | 99 |

*"Hiking is my way to meditate
while in motion — wonderful!"*

UTE LIPPOLD

The Loops

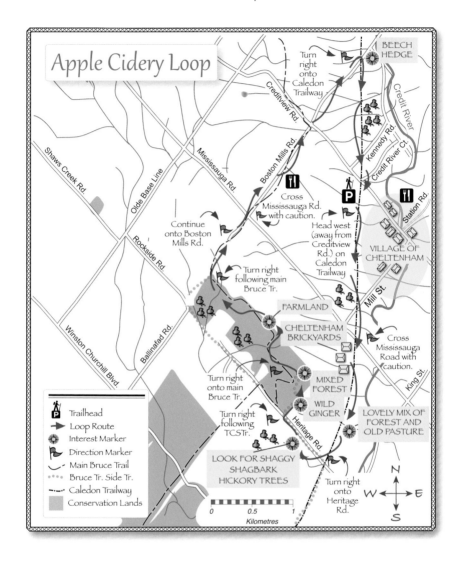

## Apple Cidery Loop

BEECH HEDGE

Turn right onto Caledon Trailway

Creditview Rd.

Credit River

Kennedy Rd.

Credit River Ct.

Mississauga Rd.

Boston Mills Rd.

Shaws Creek Rd.

Olde Base Line

Cross Mississauga Rd. with caution.

Station Rd.

Head west (away from Creditview Rd.) on Caledon Trailway

VILLAGE OF CHELTENHAM

Continue onto Boston Mills Rd.

Rockside Rd.

Turn right following main Bruce Tr.

FARMLAND

Mill St.

CHELTENHAM BRICKYARDS

Cross Mississauga Road with caution.

Winston Churchill Blvd.

Ballinafad Rd.

MIXED FOREST

King St.

Turn right onto main Bruce Tr.

WILD GINGER

LOVELY MIX OF FOREST AND OLD PASTURE

Turn right following TCSTr.

Heritage Rd.

LOOK FOR SHAGGY SHAGBARK HICKORY TREES

Turn right onto Heritage Rd.

N
W — E
S

### Legend

- 🚶 Trailhead
- ➡ Loop Route
- ✹ Interest Marker
- ⚑ Direction Marker
- ⌣ Main Bruce Trail
- •••• Bruce Tr. Side Tr.
- -·-·- Caledon Trailway
- ▨ Conservation Lands

0      0.5      1

Kilometres

*"There's something about moving at a comfortable pace through a wooded landscape that settles the soul and induces civilization-jangled nerves to uncurl and lie flat."*

DON FERGUSON

# Apple Cidery Loop
## (Cheltenham)

### Nicola's
## Insider Info

**LENGTH**
12.5 kilometres

**LEVEL OF DIFFICULTY**
Moderate

**LENGTH OF TIME**
3 to 4 hours

**NUMBER OF STEPS**
15,946

**kCAL BURNED** 663

**HIGHLIGHTS**
Cheltenham Brickyards,
wild ginger, mature
mixed hardwood forest

**PLACES TO EAT/DRINK**
Spirit Tree Estate Cidery
(closed Mon./Tues.) near
Cheltenham, Cheltenham
General Store/Peartree
B&B in Terra Cotta

**ENTRANCE FEE** n/a

**TRAILHEAD**
N43° 46.267' W79° 55.744'

## OVERVIEW

Cheltenham is actually in Caledon rather than Halton Region, but it's so close, and this is such a great loop, that I included it here. It gives Halton hikers a taste of Caledon's rocky terrain and introduces you to the wonderful Spirit Tree Estate Cidery. In addition to offering several kinds of hard and sweet ciders in its bistro, its menu includes artisanal pizzas on weekends. You can also get breads, fruit pies and everything that you could want near the end of a lovely hike, including apples and lattes. I'm particularly fond of their cookies — just call me "monster."

In the spring, this loop is blanketed with wildflowers. The mature mixed hardwood forest has shagbark hickory, blue beech, yellow birch, oak, maple, white birch, beech and basswood. There are rocky sections, as well as a short stretch of road that passes gorgeous homes shaded by a maple-tree canopy. The loop follows what was the Hamilton & North Western Railway (now the Caledon Trailway), as well as the Bruce Trail.

*Visit the Spirit Tree Estate Cidery for a perfect après-hike.* (www.spirittreecider.com)

GPS

**TRAIL MARKER**
*Loop 1*

# Directions

1. Park in the lot designated for the Caledon Trailway. It's on the west side of Creditview Rd. at the north end of the village of Cheltenham, across from Credit River Ct. It's a bit hard to find, so use the GPS coordinate included in Nicola's Insider Info.

2. Leave the parking lot by heading west on the Caledon Trailway (away from Creditview Rd.).

3. This rail trail follows the route of the Hamilton & North Western (H&NW) Railway, which linked Hamilton to Collingwood. It was the first of 2 railways that served Cheltenham, arriving in the village in 1874. Though most people thought they would bring growth, the railways were the beginning of Cheltenham's demise. Rather than shop at home, residents took the train to shop elsewhere. Over time, Cheltenham's 3 hotels, 2 distilleries, 2 mills, 4 stores, 2 taverns and other businesses closed their doors.

4. Follow the Trailway for 3.5k, crossing Mill St. before crossing Mississauga Rd. very carefully.

5. On the west side of Mississauga Rd. are the abandoned Cheltenham Brickyards, a well-known landmark. The Interprovincial Brick Co. produced its first bricks there in 1914. Carmen Delutis, who worked there from 1922 until the early 1960s, said that during WWII he was in charge of approximately 25 German prisoners of war. "They got paid — not full scale. They were good workers, and we never thought they would try to escape," he recalled. At its peak, the Interprovincial Brick Co. produced 90,000 bricks a day from 7 kilns. The Westminster Hospital in London, Ontario, and the Skyline Hotel in Toronto were constructed from these bricks. Domtar Inc. took over Interprovincial in 1928; its kilns operated until 1964 when pressed bricks replaced wire-cut ones.

6. Chinguacousy Township bought the land and buildings in 1972. The Town of Caledon took them over in 1974 and planned a park. The Town even moved a railway turnstile there so a steam train could use the old H&NW line. In 1975 however, the Town sold the land to the Ontario government to offset the cost of building the new municipal offices in Caledon East. In 1977, the Town successfully blocked provincial plans to demolish the old buildings. Unable to knock the buildings down, the province invited applications for a brick-making plant. Cheltenham residents fought the application, and, after a drawn-out fight, they won. But the citizens' victory was short-lived. They were shocked when Interprovincial submitted an application to remove

*Trees provide natural air conditioning along this stretch of trail.*

a portion of the 35 million tonnes of red clay that lies under the property. For this reason, instead of being a park and terminal for a Credit Valley steam train, the old brickyards are attached to a mining operation that remains active. To obtain its license, the company agreed to preserve the historical buildings, protect environmentally sensitive areas and rehabilitate the quarries.

7. When you come to a paved road (Heritage Rd.), turn right and follow the blue blazes of the Terra Cotta Side Tr. (TCSTr.) along the road.

8. Some 600m later, follow the blue blazes as the TCSTr. turns right and re-enters the forest.

9. After 1k along a pretty, forested trail, the TCSTr. ends at the main Bruce Tr. Turn right onto the main Bruce Tr., following its white blazes.

10. The trail goes through a beautiful forest. At first, cedar and oak dominate, but later the woods comprise maple, birch, oak, ironwood, ash, and even shagbark hickory and some yellow birch. It's a very rocky stretch of trail, but absolutely lovely.

11. After almost 2.5k, you come to a junction with the Rockside Side Tr. Turn right here, sticking with the white blazes of the main Bruce Tr.

12. In time, the trail climbs a smallish hill. On the other side, you leave the forest behind and find yourself walking along Boston Mills Rd. Follow this dirt road, cross Mississauga Rd. with extreme care and keep going on what is now a paved, albeit quiet, road.

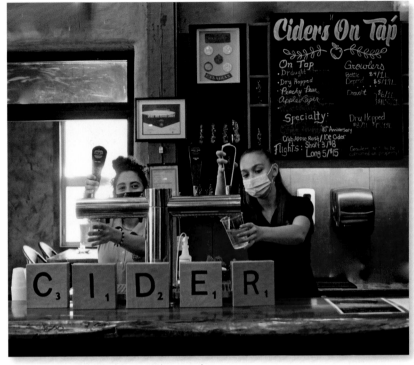

*Spirit Tree Estate Cidery, a welcome port — storm or no storm.*

13. Just up ahead, as promised, is the Spirit Tree Estate Cidery (closed Mon./Tues.). Spirit Tree grows some unusual species of cider apples and has a range of ciders for you to try. It also has a wood-fired oven that turns out pizza, bread and other baked goods. Give your tired feet a break by heading inside for a seat in the bistro.

14. Leave the cidery by turning right onto Boston Mills Rd., and continue to follow the main Bruce Tr.'s white blazes. On a clear day you'll see a great vista to your right and a few farms along this stretch.

15. Cross Creditview Rd. and keep going straight, leaving the Bruce Tr. behind.

16. A little more than 1k after crossing Creditview Rd., you come to where the Caledon Trailway crosses Boston Mills Rd. Look for the green house number sign "1869" because the Trailway is not well marked at this point. Notice the impressive beech hedge just past the Trailway entry.

17. Turn right onto the Caledon Trailway. Cross Kennedy Rd. and then Creditview Rd. before arriving at your car.

# Authors' Way Loop
## (Georgetown)

## OVERVIEW

This is a good loop if you want to get some fresh air before trying out one of downtown Georgetown's great cafés, or if you live near downtown Georgetown and want a local outing. It winds through a natural area and along some boardwalks. It connects lovely downtown Georgetown with the Chris Walker Trail. You can take a stroller, walk abreast and chat with friends, while enjoying the forested sections and oohing and aahing at Georgetown's gracious old homes. But if it's a vigorous hike in nature that you're after, leave this loop for another day.

I called this route the Authors' Way Loop because I was surprised to come across streets named after several of Canada's best-known authors. These include Berton Blvd., Mowat Crescent and Atwood Ave. Although you won't see them on this hike, the same development also has Callaghan Crescent, Munro Circle and Grey Owl Run among others. After Chris Walker's death in 2007, the city renamed the old Trafalgar Trail to commemorate this nature enthusiast since he was key to Georgetown having a network of trails.

*"I never go on a hike without my camera. I love watching for all the little details of nature and photographing an unexpected shape or a feisty little plant."*

MARCIA RUBY

## 2

### Nicola's
### Insider Info

**LENGTH**
5.9 kilometres

**LEVEL OF DIFFICULTY**
Easy

**LENGTH OF TIME**
1.5 to 2 hours

**NUMBER OF STEPS**
8,445

**kCAL BURNED** 258

**HIGHLIGHTS**
Wilderness in the city, Main Street, author-named streets

**PLACES TO EAT/DRINK**
Heather's Bakery, Silvercreek Socialhaus, The St. George Pub, Symposium Café Restaurant in Georgetown

**ENTRANCE FEE** n/a

**TRAILHEAD**
N43° 38.893'W79° 55.677'

GPS

**TRAIL MARKER**
Loop 2

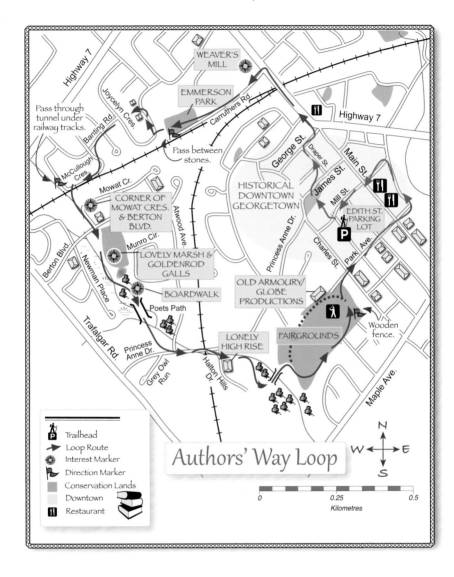

Authors' Way Loop

## Directions

1. Park near downtown Georgetown in the Edith St. parking lot at the corner of Edith and Mill Streets. There is no charge.

2. Leave the parking lot following the cinder path into Remembrance Park via a gazebo.

3. Turn right following Veterans' Walk as it parallels Princess Anne Dr.

4. Turn left onto Draper St., right onto George St. and left onto Main St. Continue north on Main St. and leave downtown. The road passes The St. George Pub and climbs over the railway tracks.

5. Just past the railway tracks, turn left onto Carruthers Rd. Walk alongside the railway tracks, and then Emmerson Park, leaving city life behind.

6. At the end of Carruthers Rd., go between the stones, following a paved path past the playground. It links with Joycelyn Cres.

7. Turn right onto Joycelyn Cres., until you come to a fire hydrant. Turn left here and follow a path between houses. At the street (also Jocelyn Cres.), turn right and then left onto Banting Rd.

8. Follow Banting Rd. until you come to McCullough Cres., where you turn left again. McCullough Cres. swings right and follows alongside the railway tracks, which are hidden behind a high fence.

9. When McCullough Cres. swings right again, you turn left and go through a pedestrian tunnel that runs under the railway tracks.

10. This paved trail, with a ravine on your right, takes you to Mowat Cres., which you follow to the stop sign.

11. At the stop sign, note that you are at the intersection of Mowat Cres. and Berton Blvd. It's hard to imagine *Never Cry Wolf* encountering *The Last Spike* at this desolate location.

12. Cross Berton Blvd. and pick up the Chris Walker Tr., which is directly across the road. Take the right fork where the cinder trail separates.

13. Suburban streets soon give way to a lovely wetland. There were birds galore, including a great blue heron.

14. I came across lots of goldenrod galls along the boardwalk. Look for these small round balls that are part of the stem. They are home to goldenrod gall flies, which do not harm the plant. They live most of their lives either in the gall or walking on the plant since they don't fly well. Downy woodpeckers peck holes in the galls and eat the insects.

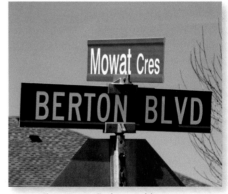

*I'm not sure Farley would approve of the font size on these signs.*

*Nature is within Georgetown.*

15. Follow the boardwalk, staying right, to a bridge. After the bridge, at a T-intersection of trails, turn left and go up the rise. It comes out onto Princess Anne Dr.

16. Go left, following Princess Anne Dr., and pass under the overpass.

17. On the other side of the overpass, turn right onto Halton Hills Dr. and then left onto a cinder path just before the lonely apartment building.

18. At the 3-way intersection of trails, turn left, re-entering the forest.

19. Pass an interpretive sign about Chris Walker and go over a small bridge. Continue along the boardwalk, looking for Canada mayflower, ferns, dame's rocket and burdock.

20. The trail climbs up a short ascent and comes to a wire fence. Pass through the open gate and find yourself in the Georgetown Fairgrounds.

21. Continue straight ahead, picking up the track (going counter-clockwise) that would once have featured standardbred racing. I liked walking around this track and thinking about the thousands of horses that would have used it. Now it seems to be a popular place for a stroll.

22. At the start of a low wooden fence on your right, leave the track. You will be across from 3rd base on the ball diamond. Head toward the building that has a green roof.

23. This is the Old Armoury, home to Globe Productions. This not-for-profit theatre company puts on 2 to 3 musicals per year using local Halton Hills talent. Chris Walker was an original member. They called themselves Globe Productions because the company began in 1964, the 400th anniversary of Shakespeare's birth.

24. Leave the fairgrounds by passing between the stone gates. You come out onto Park Ave. with its fragrant shrubs in spring.

25. Cross Charles St. and then busy Main St. Continue on Park Ave. where it drops into the river valley before bending left and going back up to Mill St.

26. Turn left onto Mill St. Cross Main St. and return to your car in the Edith St. parking lot.

27. As I mentioned in the Overview, you may want to wander through old Georgetown. There are some lovely old homes, most of them well maintained. There are lots of shops and restaurants and lattes, and because Hwy. 7 bypasses Main St., there are no big trucks or masses of speeding cars. This is one of southern Ontario's prettiest and more peaceful towns.

*One of Georgetown's many lovely homes.*

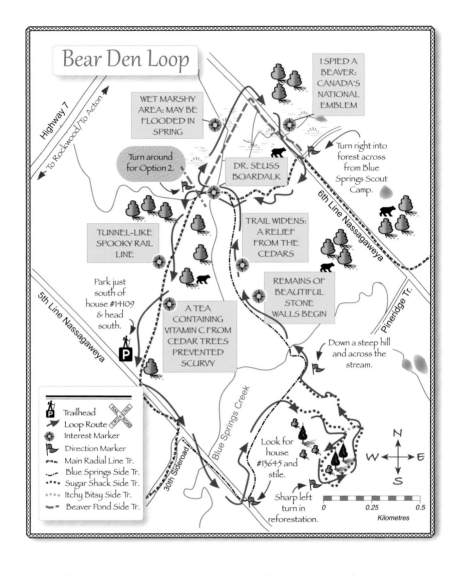

## Bear Den Loop

I SPIED A BEAVER: CANADA'S NATIONAL EMBLEM

WET MARSHY AREA: MAY BE FLOODED IN SPRING

Turn right into forest across from Blue Springs Scout Camp.

Highway 7

To Rockwood / To Acton

Turn around for Option 2.

DR. SEUSS BOARDALK

6th Line Nassagaweya

TUNNEL-LIKE SPOOKY RAIL LINE

TRAIL WIDENS: A RELIEF FROM THE CEDARS

Park just south of house #14109 & head south.

A TEA CONTAINING VITAMIN C FROM CEDAR TREES PREVENTED SCURVY

REMAINS OF BEAUTIFUL STONE WALLS BEGIN

Pineridge Tr.

5th Line Nassagaweya

Down a steep hill and across the stream.

**Legend**

- 🅿 Trailhead
- ➤ Loop Route
- ✳ Interest Marker
- ⚑ Direction Marker
- ▪▪▪ Main Radial Line Tr.
- - - Blue Springs Side Tr.
- ••• Sugar Shack Side Tr.
- •••• Itchy Bitsy Side Tr.
- ⌐ Beaver Pond Side Tr.

TRAIL CROSSING

30th Sideroad

Blue Springs Creek

Look for house #13645 and stile.

Sharp left turn in reforestation.

N
W · E
S

0    0.25    0.5
Kilometres

*"Hiking is about the entire journey, from planning the route, locating the start point, following the trail and the trail guide and finding a special place for lunch or a break to the sense of satisfaction from successfully completing the trek."*

ANN HILL

# Bear Den Loop (Acton/Rockwood)

*When I revised this guide, this loop was closed due to Covid 19, so these directions have not been updated. Check with the Guelph Hiking Trail Club (www.guelphhiking.com/RLT) for up-to-date information. • This route is best hiked in the fall when it's drier and there are fewer mosquitoes.*

## OVERVIEW

This was my first venture onto the 33.3k Guelph Radial Line Trail, which is a rail trail that runs from Guelph to Limehouse and is managed by the Guelph Hiking Trail Club (**www.guelphhiking.com**). Given my penchant for loops, I looked for and was pleased to discover this circular route in the Blue Springs Valley (Section 5). This area is very rural with lots of forests and swamps. This is a great combo for hiking, though it's a bit buggy during the summer. The loop crosses land known as the Bear Den that was donated to The Nature Conservancy of Canada by Jesse Mackenzie, Dalziel Glynn and Sandy Agnew.

Opened in 1917, the Guelph Radial Line ran successfully until events conspired against it, and in 1931 the Canadian National Railway shut it down. The Guelph club notes the line operated at speeds up to 130kph! Most rail trails are wide open and obviously railbeds. This one is completely different. Cedars have grown up, and in places you feel as though you are walking through an enchanted forest. It's spooky and it has a wonderful Dr. Seuss-like boardwalk.

If you've wondered about the Guelph Radial Line Trail, check out this loop.

**Nicola's**
## Insider Info

**LENGTH**
7.5 kilometres
(5.5k option)

**LEVEL OF DIFFICULTY**
Easy

**LENGTH OF TIME**
1.75 to 2.5 hours
(1.5 to 2 hours)

**NUMBER OF STEPS**
9,368

**kCAL BURNED** 295

**HIGHLIGHTS**
A beaver! Dr. Seuss-like boardwalk, cedar forest, old railbed

**PLACES TO EAT/DRINK**
Eramosa River Café (closed Sun.),
Heaven on 7 Bistro & Pub (closed Mon./Tues.) in Rockwood

**ENTRANCE FEE** n/a

**TRAILHEAD**
N43° 36.201'W80° 05.794'

**TRAIL MARKER**
*Loop 3*

*One of many remains of stone walls along this loop.*

# Directions

1. There is enough parking for 1 or 2 cars at the northernmost trail entrance on 5th Line, a little south of house number sign "14109". It's just south of Hwy. 7, between Acton and Rockwood.

2. Begin by walking south (away from Hwy. 7) along 5th Line. Following the orange blazes of the main Guelph Radial Line Tr., pass 30th Sideroad and cross a bridge over Blue Springs Creek. As you climb out of the valley, look for house number sign "13645". Just past it, there's a stile over a fence on your left. This is the Blue Springs Side Tr., and it's marked with blue blazes.

3. Climb the stile and follow a trail, which was overgrown when I walked it, between 2 fences. After about 700m, you enter a forest and there are signs for the Sugar Shack Side Tr.

4. Turn right, going into the forest on the Sugar Shack Side Tr., passing through a couple of reforested areas. At the bottom of a gentle slope in the 2nd one, just before a path leaves the forest, the trail makes a sharp left turn. It's easy to miss.

5. The forest is really thick. There's a lot of undergrowth — hence the mosquitoes — and evidence that this land was farmed not long ago: the remains of old stone walls as well as the odd large maple tree with a broad canopy that indicates it grew in the open as opposed to in a forest where it's all about growing tall and slim.

6. Some 500m later, there's a Y-intersection of trails. The short and buggy, cleverly named Itchy Bitsy Side Tr. veers left, but you go right, staying on the Blue Springs Side Tr. Both have blue blazes.

7. In 400m, there's another trail intersection where you veer right again, and then head down a steep hill and over a creek.

8. The trail widens and is almost road-like. Normally, I like narrow trails, but in this case I found the wider path a nice change, maybe because of all the undergrowth. Look along here for the remains of what must have been

*This long boardwalk is Dr. Seuss-like. My compliments to the builders.*

lovely stone walls. These walls collapse because they are built with small wooden wedges to keep them solid. Over time, the wood rots and the wall falls down.

9. When you arrive at the end of the Blue Springs Side Tr., turn left onto the further left of 2 trails marked with orange blazes. This is the main Radial Line Tr. (If you come to the Porcupine Hut you are on the wrong trail.)

10. Watch for a boardwalk to your left in the dense vegetation. Take it, crossing a stream and enjoying this Dr. Seuss-like boardwalk, which continues for a long time through the cedar forest. I love boardwalks, but I love this one more than most. Whoever built it made it all winding with rounded sides. It's very cool — if a bit slippery. And, if you take the Beaver Pond Side Tr., you get to walk over it for a 2nd time!

11. At the end of the boardwalk you have a choice to make. You can return to your car here, or you can add the 2k-long Beaver Pond Side Tr. As an incentive to take the longer route, not only will you get to walk along the boardwalk again, but I saw a beaver on the Beaver Pond Side Tr. How neat is that?

## Longer Option (7.5k total hike)

12. Turn right onto the Beaver Pond Side Tr. and follow it for 650m along the old, overgrown railbed. In places you are almost walking through a tunnel.

13. When you arrive at 6th Line, turn right. After about 400m, the trail re-enters the forest, right across the road from the Blue Springs Scout Camp. This is the terminus of the Beaver Pond Side Tr.

14. Enter the forest and veer right, following the orange blazes of the main Radial Line Tr. The wide trail is in a mature cedar forest. If you come to a blue sign for the Archery Range, turn back. You missed a left turn at the bottom of the hill.

15. When you arrive back at the terminus of the Blue Springs Side Tr., veer right, following the orange blazes of the main Radial Line Tr. Go over the creek and onto the Dr. Seuss boardwalk again.

16. At the end of the boardwalk, turn left this time and follow the main Radial Line Tr. It's another 650m to your car.

## Shorter Option (5.5k total hike)

1. Continued from Point #11 above.

2. At the end of the boardwalk, turn left and follow the main Radial Line Tr. It's another 650m to your car.

# Burlington Beach Route

## OVERVIEW

I phoned the Waterfront Regeneration Trust and Vicki Barron, the director of administration, answered the phone. She encouraged me to consider a route from Burlington's Spencer Smith Park to the border with Hamilton at the Burlington Canal. She assured me it would make me appreciate the trail that stretches for more than 1,600k along several Canadian lakes. "Beach, lots of beach," promised Vicki.

And do you know what? Vicki was absolutely right. Not only is there a kilometre-long beach on this in-and-out route, but it is actually treated like a beach. There were people in bikinis and families having picnics. There were children making sandcastles and people swimming, sailing and paddleboarding.

If you like to walk barefoot in the sand but can't make it to the West Indies, this hike is for you. And there are lots of nearby cafés. This was the last route I completed for the first version of this guide, so I celebrated with a creamy latte. Then I visited MollyCake, went to A Different Drummer Books, and realized that there are some serious rewards for hikers in Burlington.

*"I never know what I shall encounter."*

LYNNE NORMAN

Locals favour lattes at the **Lakeshore Coffee House.** *Find out why.* (www.lakeshorecoffeehouse.com)

## Nicola's Insider Info

**LENGTH**
5.6 kilometres

**LEVEL OF DIFFICULTY**
Easy

**LENGTH OF TIME**
1.5 to 2 hours

**NUMBER OF STEPS**
8,016

**kCAL BURNED** 245

**HIGHLIGHTS**
The beach, cafés, waterfowl, lattes

**PLACES TO EAT/DRINK**
How about gelato at Crema di Gelato (closed Mon), gluten-free meals at the LettuceLove Café (closed Mon.), beach grub at Three Bills or a latte at the Lakeshore Coffee House? You can pick up an amazing cake at MollyCake (closed Mon.).

**ENTRANCE FEE** n/a

**TRAILHEAD**
N43° 19.458'W79° 47.770'

GPS

**TRAIL MARKER**
Loop 4

Burlington Beach Route

# Directions

1. Park near the intersection of Brant St. and Lakeshore Rd. in downtown Burlington. Cross Lakeshore Rd. at the lights at Brant St. and look for a set of stone stairs that head down to the waterfront on the right side of the Waterfront Hotel Downtown Burlington.

2. Head out to the spaceship-like structure on the Brant Street Pier. From this vantage point, you can see the distant turnaround point of the hike, just before the large bridge that spans the Burlington Canal.

*This viewer actually worked.*

3. After a look around the pier, head toward the bridge (west) along the pedestrian Naval Veterans Promenade that follows the shoreline of Lake Ontario. There is a gazebo and washroom on your right. I stopped in at the memorial that's dedicated to naval veterans and their ships and was moved by "The Old Sailor" poem. Take a few minutes here. This is a sightseeing route, so enjoy what it has to offer.

4. Continue following the lakeshore, passing by or stopping in at Three Bills restaurant. I detoured out to a lookout that had one of those 25-cent magnifying viewers and dropped in a coin to have a look-see at the still-distant bridge. I also read about the victory at Burlington Bay in 1813 when Sir James Yeo out-manoeuvred his American foe, thereby preserving British dominance on Lake Ontario.

5. Continue along the waterfront as the trail turns left and becomes more shaded. When you get the opportunity to veer onto the beach, do so. Kick off your shoes and enjoy that most enjoyable foot experience.

6. The beach is narrow, but there are lots of picnic tables and plentiful oaks and other leafy trees that, unlike palm trees, provide great shady spots for eating or reading or observing. Lots of people were out doing exactly what people do at beaches: sunbathing, swimming, paddleboarding, sailing and making sandcastles. I'm not sure what I expected, but it wasn't Burlington, West Indies!

*Gulls enjoy the beach as much as people do.*

7. Pass by the Burlington Beach Catamaran Club (no sign, but usually there are kayaks out front) and look for stairs to your right. Take the stairs, leaving the beach.

*The spaceship-like structure on the Brant Street Pier.*

8.  Turn right and walk back along a nicely shaded path that is slightly removed from the beach, or you can retrace your walk in the sand. It's your choice.

9.  When you come to a spot just before the naval memorial where a paved trail goes left past a couch made from stone, follow the paved trail past the couch, going behind the gazebo and nearer the washroom. This path leads you back to the stone stairs beside the Waterfront Hotel Downtown Burlington and Brant St.

10. Your hike ends here, right where your coffee, gelato and cake adventures begin.

# Burlington Waterfront/ Nicola's Folly Loop

## OVERVIEW

I've rated this loop as easy, but the day I walked it, it proved to be anything but. In the end, though, I discovered a very nice hike with a beautiful walk along a stretch of the lakeshore between Burlington and Oakville. It loops into a few parks and along a creek that runs through a peaceful forest. You'll walk along quiet streets, and you'll pass by some lovely homes.

My day was challenging because I walked more than 20k in the heat to come up with this 5.3k route. My folly became more grievous because I forgot to take any money and ran out of water. Trusting the Waterfront Trail (**www.waterfronttrail. org**) map, I blithely selected a route that ended up involving an 8k stretch along busy Lakeshore Road. There were 4 lanes of cars whizzing by me. Some hike. It was awful. Walk the Waterfront Trail, but avoid the stretch between Spencer Smith Park and Burloak Regional Waterfront Park. Rest assured, this loop does NOT include that stretch of hiker hell.

*"I haven't yet discovered a trail where I've said afterwards, 'Sure wasted my time on this one!'"*

JOYCE McGLINCHEY

## Nicola's Insider Info

**LENGTH**
5.3 kilometres

**LEVEL OF DIFFICULTY**
Easy

**LENGTH OF TIME**
1.5 to 2 hours

**NUMBER OF STEPS**
6,834

**kCAL BURNED** 187

**HIGHLIGHTS**
Waterfront

**PLACES TO EAT/DRINK**
According to TripAdvisor, the following are the 5 best cafés in Burlington: LettuceLove Café, Saving Thyme, Kelly's Bake Shoppe, Lola's Choco Bar and Sweet House, and the Lakeshore Coffee House.

**ENTRANCE FEE**
n/a

**TRAILHEAD**
N43° 22.147′ W79° 43.665′

GPS

**TRAIL MARKER**
Loop 5

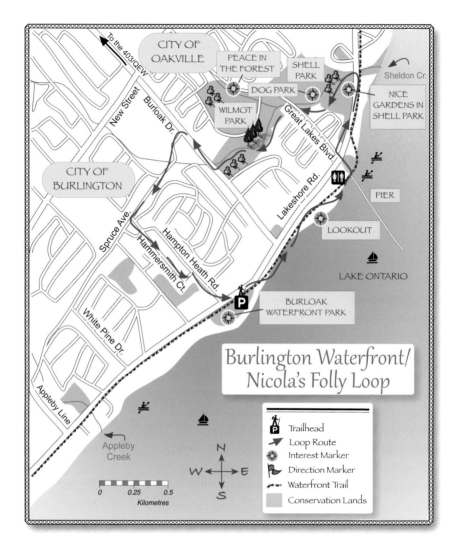

Burlington Waterfront/
Nicola's Folly Loop

**Legend:**
- Trailhead
- Loop Route
- Interest Marker
- Direction Marker
- Waterfront Trail
- Conservation Lands

0    0.25    0.5
Kilometres

N W E S

## Directions

1. Park in the Burloak Waterfront Park, which you access from Lakeshore Rd., west of Burloak Dr.

2. Look for a paved trail that heads east (to your left if you are looking toward Lake Ontario). Follow it onto Lakeshore Rd. for a bit but don't be dismayed, it quickly leaves the road, along a trail that passes through yellow barriers and goes behind a large apartment complex. I saw kayakers on the lake here.

*I envied these folks.*

3.  Follow the trail veering right. Eventually you arrive at a parking lot near a long pier where there are washrooms.

4.  Read the interpretive sign about Harry Barrett. It was Barrett who noticed the clause in *Ontario's Planning Act* that has allowed the Waterfront Tr. to access the shoreline. I silently thanked Mr. Barrett. Sadly though — as I found out — his contribution has not yet extended to a large part of Burlington's waterfront.

5.  Turn left in this parking lot and cross Lakeshore Rd. at the traffic lights for Great Lakes Blvd. Turn right and follow Lakeshore Rd. for a short distance until you come to the entrance to Shell Park. Enter the park and take a few moments to admire the gardens. Then turn left into a parking lot. Continue walking to the back of the park, passing by a skateboard park, then another parking lot and then a large fenced area for off-leash dogs. It's fun to watch them play.

6.  Pass by the off-leash dog area along a vague path in the grass. The dog park will be on your right. Continue walking until you come to Great Lakes Blvd., where you turn right onto the street. After a short 100m, metal guardrails appear on both sides of the street. Cross the street and just before the guardrails, look for some mailboxes. To the left of them is a trail. Follow it.

*I put my money on the paddleboard.*

7. You enter a forest with a creek to your right. I felt a profound sense of relief when I got here. Nice as the waterfront was, it lacks the calming effect of a forest. In fact, "forest bathing" has become a cornerstone of preventive medicine in Japan, according to the *shinrin-yoku* website. This company offers a 1.5k-walk that takes 2 to 3 hours to complete. They charge $30 for this service — the same price as this hiking guide!

*What part of "off-road" does the Waterfront Trail not understand?*

8. Follow this trail until it comes to Burloak Dr. Turn right onto Burloak Dr. and walk up to Spruce Ave. Turn left onto this quiet street.

9. After 700m, turn left onto Hampton Heath Rd. When it veers left, stay straight on the quieter Hammersmith Ct. When it ends, turn right back onto Hampton Heath Rd. At the stop sign, cross Lakeshore Rd. and turn left, following it back to Burloak Waterfront Park where your car is parked.

# Crawford Lake Loop
## (Campbellville)

## OVERVIEW

The 468ha Crawford Lake Conservation Area is a gem. Its primary features are its 19k network of trails and the beautiful and unique Crawford Lake, but make sure you visit the Iroquoian village where you may be able to handle bear, beaver, wolf, skunk and other furs. Crawford Lake is a meromictic lake: its surface water does not mix with the deeper water. It may have been formed when an enormous sinkhole filled with water. Then again, it may have been created by a process known as hydraulic mining. The trail passes by marvelous carvings, each featuring a different species at risk; follows along the top of the escarpment ridge and has several places where you look out over the Nassagaweya Canyon and the Milton Outlier. It includes The Moccasin Walk, which follows a lovely Indigenous poem called "Grandmother Moon."

In the late 1800s, the Crawfords purchased what is now the conservation area. The family built a lumber mill and an elegant house that became their summer retreat. The lake, originally known as Little Lake, was turned into a trout preserve, although today you'll find only smallmouth bass in its waters.

> **Conservation Halton**
> (www.conservationhalton.ca) *encourages you and your family to enjoy the trails at all of our parks.*

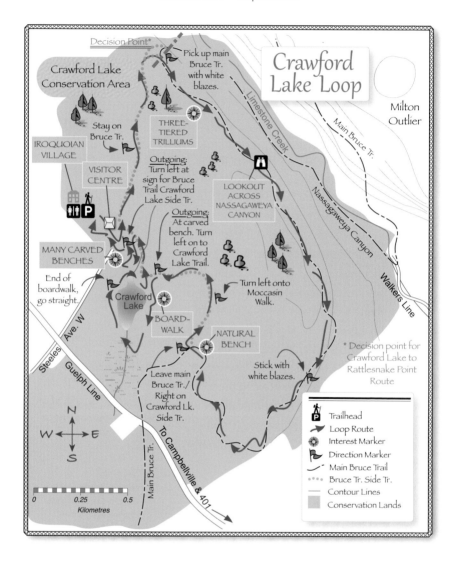

## Crawford Lake Loop

Decision Point*

Crawford Lake Conservation Area

Pick up main Bruce Tr. with white blazes.

Milton Outlier

Main Bruce Tr.

Limestone Creek

THREE-TIERED TRILLIUMS

Stay on Bruce Tr.

IROQUOIAN VILLAGE

VISITOR CENTRE

Outgoing: Turn left at sign for Bruce Trail Crawford Lake Side Tr.

LOOKOUT ACROSS NASSAGAWEYA CANYON

Nassagaweya Canyon

Outgoing: At carved bench. Turn left on to Crawford Lake Trail.

MANY CARVED BENCHES

Walkers Line

End of boardwalk, go straight.

Turn left onto Moccasin Walk.

Crawford Lake

BOARD-WALK

NATURAL BENCH

* Decision point for Crawford Lake to Rattlesnake Point Route

Steeles Ave. W

Guelph Line

Stick with white blazes.

Leave main Bruce Tr./ Right on Crawford Lk. Side Tr.

Main Bruce Tr.

To Campbellville & 401

N
W E
S

### Legend
- **Trailhead**
- **Loop Route**
- **Interest Marker**
- **Direction Marker**
- **Main Bruce Trail**
- **Bruce Tr. Side Tr.**
- **Contour Lines**
- **Conservation Lands**

0      0.25      0.5
Kilometres

*"By hiking in this area, it reminds me of the quality
of the natural environment in which we are lucky enough
to be living. We all want more, but by living here,
we already have more than most."*

MIKE VASELENAK

# Directions

*At the time of writing, there were plans to change the trail markings and colour code system along this route. • Currently, you require a reservation to visit the Crawford Lake Conservation Area. You can book two-hour slots at **www.conservationhalton.ca.***

1. Park in the Crawford Lake Conservation Area. Make your way to the Visitor Centre. On the far, downhill side of the Visitor Centre, look for a large sign that says "Greenbelt Walks/Crawford Lake Conservation Area/Trailhead." If you nip into the Visitor Centre, you can pick up a trail map, which will be helpful, though it may not be up to date.

2. Go past this sign, following the paved path down a gentle slope.

3. After a short 100m, turn left at an intersection of trails, following the blue blazes of the Bruce Tr.'s Crawford Lake Side Tr. A sign says the trail goes to Rattlesnake Point, but don't worry, you won't be going that far.

4. At the next trail intersection, go straight, following the blue blazes.

5. Look for a little unmarked trail to your left that goes into an old ruin. It's near an amazing old stone wall made from enormous rocks.

6. At the next fork in the trail, go right, still following the blue blazes of the Crawford Lake Side Tr. Bypass the Canyon Bypass Side Tr.

7. When you come to the next trail intersection, go right, picking up the white blazes of the main Bruce Tr. (To go to Rattlesnake Point, take the Crawford Lake to Rattlesnake Route on page 51.)

8. The trail follows along the top of the escarpment for almost 2k. There are great views of Rattlesnake Point.

9. Stick with the white blazes of the main Bruce Tr., passing by the Escarpment Tr. I came across a very odd trillium along here (see photo). Rather than having 3 green leaves, then a 3-lobed white flower with 3 green sepals, it had 3 tiers of 3 green leaves.

*I came across this unusual 3-tiered trillium near the canyon.*

10. At the lookout, interpretive signs explain what the Milton Outlier is and how the Nassagaweya Canyon was formed. They also give information about turkey vultures, large birds that you will very likely see soaring overhead if you walk this route between April and October. They nest in the cliffs to keep their young safe from predators and because they like the updraft caused by the cliff.

11. Continue along the clifftop, following the white blazes. Gradually, the cliffs become a steep hill and then a not-so-steep hill and then the trail leaves the rocky terrain that is so common along the escarpment.

12. Stay with the white blazes until you come to a T-intersection. Turn right here, following a path that is now cinder-covered. This is the Crawford Lake Side Tr., and it is marked with the blue blazes of a Bruce Tr. side trail. You leave the main Bruce Tr. here.

13. At the next trail intersection, turn left onto The Moccasin Walk (still part of the Crawford Lake Side Tr.), where you will be following an Indigenous poem called "Grandmother Moon." It's a very peaceful forest, and I loved the poem.

*This is a view of the Milton Outlier across the Nassagaweya Canyon.*
*The Milton Outlier was separated from the main Niagara Escarpment by rivers.*

*Crawford Lake is a meromictic lake, which means its surface water does not mix with the deeper water. As a result, the sediment in the bottom of the lake is unchanged. Pollen from the 1300s has been found there.* PHOTO BY NICK MARSHALL

14. After 250m, you come to a fantastic carved wooden bench that virtually forms a barrier in front of you. Now you're in for more treats.

15. Pass by the carved bench where you will turn left onto the boardwalk. First though, I suggest you take the boardwalk that goes down to Lake Crawford, so you can look at this fabulous meromictic lake and read the interpretive signs to see what that means. You'll wonder if you are in Muskoka.

16. Back at the bench, going left on the boardwalk takes you all the way around Crawford Lake on the Crawford Lake Tr. It has blue markers (not blue blazes).

17. Crawford Lake dates back more than 10,000 years and was formed either from hydraulic mining or when a sinkhole filled with water. Interpretive signs describe these 2 processes. Also read about how the bottom of this lake doesn't support any life. Its undisturbed sediments were key to the discovery of the Iroquoian village that you will visit later.

18. Keep your eyes open for a fabulously twisted cedar tree. Sadly, it's at risk of having to be cut down since it is not doing well, according to Halton Conservation.

19. The 1k-long Crawford Lake Tr. returns to the carved bench. Turn left at the bench and follow the blue blazes of the Bruce Tr.'s Crawford Lake Side Tr.

*One of the many incredible carvings in the park.*

*This fabulously twisted cedar tree is at risk of having to be cut down.*

20. At the next T-intersection of trails, go left, continuing to follow blue blazes.

21. At the next T-intersection, go left for a 3rd time, briefly leaving the Crawford Lake Side Tr. and its blue blazes. This is an in-and-out trail that goes past a collection of amazing wooden carvings. Each of them depicts a species at risk. They are all at least fabulous and some are "fantabulous" or something better than really good.

22. When you come to the lake, turn around and return to the Crawford Lake Side Tr., where you go straight. Next you arrive at the paved path that you took at the very beginning of the hike. At the signpost, turn right, following a paved trail that climbs up to the Visitor Centre.

23. Follow it up to the Visitor Centre, where I suggest you go in the back door and up the stairs to the washrooms and gift shop.

24. Leave the Visitor Centre from the upper entrance. Turn right and take this opportunity to wander through the Iroquoian village. It's great. I particularly loved feeling the furs, and I liked the strings of corncobs up high in the ceiling.

25. Leave the Iroquoian village and return to your car.

# Crawford Lake to Rattlesnake Point Route
## (Campbellville)

*For the longer route, you will need to use the maps for the Crawford Lake to Rattlesnake Point Route and the Crawford Lake Loop on page 45.*

## OVERVIEW

This hike has it all. If you do it as an in-and-out (12.9k), it's fantastic. If you combine it with a look at the wooden carvings and a stroll around Crawford Lake, it's even better. Either way, you have a peaceful walk along the floor of the Nassagaweya Canyon within a cathedral of hardwood trees, and vista upon vista from Rattlesnake Point.

My friends Elizabeth and Sandra accompanied me on this hike on a lovely day in May. They offered some valuable feedback as to how to make this the best loop possible. We had fun oohing and aahing at the great views from Rattlesnake Point. We were hushed by the peace in the canyon and had a memorable lunch sitting with our legs dangling over the cliff face watching turkey vultures at eye level. Despite there being a plethora of trails in the Rattlesnake Point Conservation Area, none could compete with the Bruce Trail, so we agreed that this section was best done as an in-and-out along the cliff edge. I added the Leech Porter Side Trail later.

**Conservation Halton**
(**www.conservationhalton.ca**) *encourages you and your family to enjoy the trails at all of our parks.*

## 7

### Nicola's
## Insider Info

**LENGTH**
19 kilometres
(12.9k option)

**LEVEL OF DIFFICULTY**
Moderate

**LENGTH OF TIME**
4.5 to 6.5 hours
(3 to 4.5 hours)

**NUMBER of STEPS** 27,197

**kCAL BURNED** 831

**HIGHLIGHTS**
Vistas, canyon, rock climbers, crevices, Nassagaweya Canyon, Milton Outlier, carvings, Iroquoian village

**PLACES TO EAT/DRINK**
Park Visitor Centre/Flying Monkey Bike Shop & Coffee Bar, The Trail Eatery in Campbellville/Lowville Bistro in Lowville

**ENTRANCE FEE**
Adult $9.50/Senior (65+) $7.50/Child (5–14) $6.50/Child (<5) free

**HOURS**  Park opens at 8:30am daily/Buildings open at 10am daily

**TRAILHEAD**
N43° 28.191'W79° 57.071'

**BRUCE TRAIL MAP** 11

**TRAIL MARKER**
Loop 7

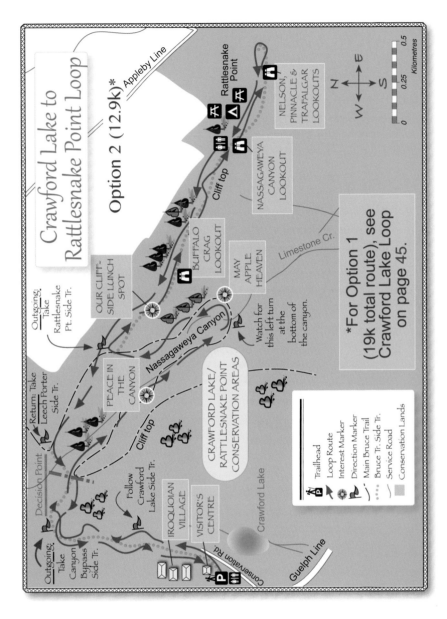

## Crawford Lake to Rattlesnake Point Loop

### Option 2 (12.9k)*

Appleby Line

Rattlesnake Point

NELSON, PINNACLE & TRAFALGAR LOOKOUTS

NASSAGAWEYA CANYON LOOKOUT

Cliff top

Limestone Cr.

BUFFALO CRAG LOOKOUT

OUR CLIFF-SIDE LUNCH SPOT

MAY APPLE HEAVEN

Watch for this left turn at the bottom of the canyon.

*For Option 1 (19k total route), see Crawford Lake Loop on page 45.

Outgoing: Take Rattlesnake Pt. Side Tr.

Return: Take Leech Porter Side Tr.

PEACE IN THE CANYON

Nassagaweya Canyon

Cliff top

CRAWFORD LAKE/ RATTLESNAKE POINT CONSERVATION AREAS

Decision Point

Follow Crawford Lake Side Tr.

Crawford Lake

**Legend**
- Trailhead
- Loop Route
- Direction Marker
- Main Bruce Trail
- Bruce Tr. Side Tr.
- Service Road
- Conservation Lands

IROQUOIAN VILLAGE

VISITOR'S CENTRE

Outgoing: Take Canyon Bypass Side Tr.

Conservation Rd.

Guelph Line

*"We particularly like to hike in the fall when the air is crisp and the smell of the damp leaves fills the air. The paths wind up and down and are a cushion of pine needles under foot."*

SANDY RICE

# Directions

*Fissures run parallel to the cliff face along much of this rocky terrain.* PHOTO BY ELIZABETH GANONG

1. Park in the Crawford Lake Conservation Area. Make your way to the Visitor Centre. On the far, downhill side of the Visitor Centre, look for a large sign that says, "Greenbelt Walks/Crawford Lake Conservation Area/Trailhead." If you nip into the Visitor Centre, you can pick up a trail map, which will be helpful.

2. Go past this sign, following the paved path down a gentle slope.

3. After a short 100m, turn left at an intersection of trails, following the blue blazes of the Bruce Tr.'s Crawford Lake Side Tr. A sign says "To Rattlesnake Point."

4. At the next trail intersection, go straight, still following blue blazes.

5. When we walked this route, the forest was full of jack-in-the-pulpits and other ephemeral spring flowers, including blue cohosh, trilliums, hepatica and more. A real treat.

6. When you come to the Canyon Bypass Side Tr., take it, following its blue blazes and leaving the Crawford Lake Side Tr. behind. It's a gentler way down, which is especially important in icy conditions. You will return by a steeper route.

7. At the end of the Canyon Bypass Side Tr., go straight ahead onto the main Bruce Tr., following its white blazes for the next 2k. This is a fabulous section of trail, and I advise walking it early in the morning. The trees down in the canyon seem unusually tall as though they are stretching to reach the sunshine. The tone is hushed, almost meditative. Pass by the Leech Porter Side Tr.

8. It's believed the word "Nassagaweya" was derived from the Anishinaabe (Ojibwa) word "nazhesahgewayyong," which means "river with 2 outlets." This area is home to waterways that drain into both the Lake Ontario and the Grand River watershed.

9. At the valley bottom, you switchback over a stream called Limestone Creek. This turn is easy to miss, even with a sign pointing toward the Bruce Tr. You are now going through mayapple heaven and will start the gentle climb out of the canyon.

10. We noted that the cedar trees through this area had exposed roots and wondered if, over time, erosion during spring runoff had washed away the soil underneath the trees.

11. Before you come to the top of the canyon, the Rattlesnake Point Side Tr. exits to your right. Take it, following its blue blazes.

12. We discovered some large morels near here. I'm not an expert, but I know enough to not give away my mushroom locations, so I'm being intentionally vague with this description.

13. Orange, yellow and red markers for the Rattlesnake Point Conservation Area trails begin to appear, but stick with the blue blazes of the Rattlesnake Point Side Tr. It's the most picturesque. Follow it all the way to Rattlesnake Point, which is a scenic 2.5k away.

14. The first viewing spot is the Buffalo Crag Lookout. There are signposts, but nothing that says "Buffalo Crag Lookout." We thought we were at Rattlesnake Point. Take a breather here, and then continue on, following the blue blazes to several more scenic lookouts.

15. Look for 400- to 800-year-old Eastern white cedars. In the 1500s, cedar trees, which are also known as the "tree of life," saved the lives of Jacques Cartier and his crew. The Iroquois showed them how to extract what turned out to be ascorbic acid, or vitamin C, from leaves and bark, thereby producing a cure for scurvy. With luck, you may also see rock climbers.

16. Soon you come to the Nassagaweya Canyon Lookout, which has washrooms, a picnic area and campsites. You are now in the Rattlesnake Point Conservation Area. I like the story about how Rattlesnake Point received its name. Some say, that in the 1800s, sailors who jumped ship in Hamilton Harbour came to this location to watch their ships leave without them. While there are no rattlesnakes there now, these men said they found hundreds of them sunning on the rocks.

17. Next up are the Nelson, Pinnacle and Trafalgar Lookouts. Take a walk down the stairs that are nearest the Pinnacle Lookout to get a closer view of the valley below and the cave-like formation in the cliff face.

18. You could follow the yellow markers of the Buffalo Crag Tr. back to the Buffalo Crag Lookout, but I suggest just turning around and retracing your footsteps along the Rattlesnake Point Side Tr. with its blue blazes. My companions and I all agreed it was worth doing it twice.

*May is morel month.*

19. When you return to the main Bruce Tr., turn right and climb up, following white blazes. After 1k, you come to the 830m-long Leech Porter Side Tr. Turn left and follow its blue blazes down a steeper, more direct route along a boardwalk to the canyon floor.

20. This side trail ends at the main Bruce Tr. Turn right at this T-intersection, following white blazes as the trail leads you up the other side of the canyon and back toward the Crawford Lake Conservation Area.

21. Stick with the main Bruce Tr. as it goes up a steeper, rockier route than the one you came down on. It's short and pretty.

22. When you come to a blue Bruce Tr. sign for the Crawford Lake Side Tr., you have a decision to make.

## You have 2 options:

### Longer Option (19k total hike)

1. Turn left, following the white blazes of the main Bruce Tr.
2. Turn to page 53 of the Crawford Lake Loop and continue from Point #8 onward, switching to the Crawford Lake Loop map.

### Shorter Option (12.9k total hike)

1. Turn right, following the Crawford Lake Side Tr. and its blue blazes, retracing your footsteps of earlier in the day.
2. When you come to a T-intersection of trails and a signpost, turn right, following the paved trail that climbs up to the Visitor Centre. After a stop at the Visitor Centre, visit the reconstructed Iroquoian village. It's well worth it.

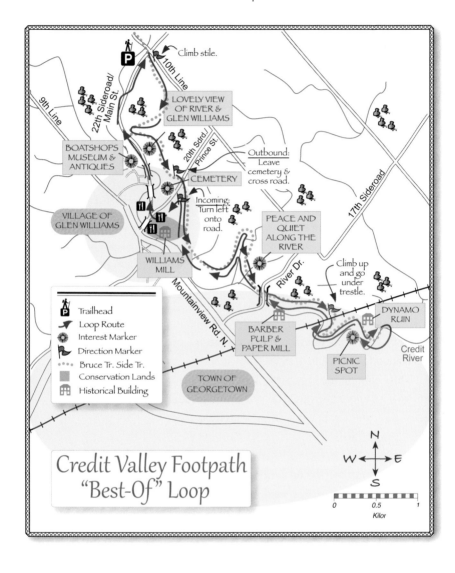

Climb stile.

**LOVELY VIEW OF RIVER & GLEN WILLIAMS**

**BOATSHOPS MUSEUM & ANTIQUES**

**CEMETERY**

Outbound: Leave cemetery & cross road.

**VILLAGE OF GLEN WILLIAMS**

Incoming: Turn left onto road.

**PEACE AND QUIET ALONG THE RIVER**

**WILLIAMS MILL**

Climb up and go under trestle.

**DYNAMO RUIN**

**BARBER PULP & PAPER MILL**

Credit River

**PICNIC SPOT**

**TOWN OF GEORGETOWN**

9th Line
10th Line
22nd Sideroad/ Main St.
20th Sdrd./ Prince St.
17th Sideroad
River Dr.
Mountainview Rd. N.

**Legend**

🥾 Trailhead
➤ Loop Route
✹ Interest Marker
⚑ Direction Marker
•••• Bruce Tr. Side Tr.
▢ Conservation Lands
⌂ Historical Building

# Credit Valley Footpath "Best-Of" Loop

N
W — E
S

0    0.5    1
Kilor

"For me, the best antidote for the grumps
is to put on my hiking boots and head for the forest.
It reminds me to be where my feet are."

GAIL GRANT

# Credit Valley Footpath "Best-Of" Loop (Glen Williams)

*Some sections of this trail flood in early spring.*

## OVERVIEW

This route sticks to the best section of the Credit Valley Footpath (CVF) and throws in the village of Glen Williams so you can add a beer or a coffee or lunch or great art to the plethora of other reasons for following this loop. And don't forget the boat museum and the antique store. What more could you want from a hike? Mountains shmountains! You get a great trail, a fabulous river, Canada's first industrial hydro-electric plant, trees, flowers, birds, beers, baked goods, lunch and more.

This beautiful section of the CVF is part of an initiative spearheaded by Credit Valley Conservation. Plans are underway to link southern Ontario's Greenbelt to Lake Ontario along the "Credit Valley Trail." Some 113k long when it's complete, it will follow the historic Credit River from its source just north of Orangeville to where it drains into Lake Ontario at Port Credit. The 90k-long Credit River was so named by the Mississaugas of the Credit First Nation, who once purchased supplies on "credit" before heading up river to gather furs. Make a day of this hike by allowing time to explore Glen Williams.

*If you want to enjoy hiking in Halton from your doorstep, contact Jill Johnson at Royal LePage Meadowtowne Realty (905-873-5592). Read about her hiking for charity activities at www.jilljohnson.ca.*

## Nicola's Insider Info

**LENGTH**
14.6 kilometres

**LEVEL OF DIFFICULTY**
Moderate

**LENGTH OF TIME**
3.5 to 5 hours

**NUMBER OF STEPS**
20,898

**kCAL BURNED** 706

**HIGHLIGHTS**
Glen Williams Cemetery, Williams Mill Visual Arts Centre, Barber Paper Mill ruins, the Credit River valley

**PLACES TO EAT/DRINK**
Kit's Little Kitchen (closed Mon. & Tues.) The Glen Tavern (closed Sun. & Mon.), Copper Kettle Pub in Glen Williams

**ENTRANCE FEE**
n/a

**TRAILHEAD**
N43° 39.736'W79° 54.506'

GPS

**TRAIL MARKER**
Loop 8

# Directions

1. Park at the intersection of 22nd Sideroad and 10th Line in Halton Hills. Much of the land in this area is owned by Sheridan Nurseries, so rows of trees and bushes fill the fields. There is no designated parking area, but the shoulder is wide in several places.

2. Head west on 22nd Sideroad (the hill will be on your left). Almost immediately, you see a blue Bruce Tr. sign and a stile on the left (south) side of the road. Climb the stile and head straight ahead, up the slope on a lane. In about 100m, you reach a well-worn trail that veers left and heads uphill. Take it.

3. This is the beginning of a 7k stretch of the Credit Valley Footpath (CVF) that follows the Credit River. It's marked by the blue blazes of a Bruce Tr. side trail.

4. For the next 30 minutes, you walk along a path that is high above the river, but just below the top of the valley. Look for some lovely, lacy old Eastern hemlocks and nice views of the Credit River below (foliage allowing). You soon see houses that are part of pretty Glen Williams.

5. The trail skirts the Glen Williams cemetery, arriving at a stile onto 20th Sideroad/Prince St. It's worth exploring the graveyard.

6. Cross the road (20th Sideroad/Prince St.) and pick up the trail's blue blazes as it continues straight ahead.

7. Pass by a subdivision on your left before the trail lands you on a suburban street. The trail continues across the road to the right, but it's a bit tricky to see the blazes. Now the trail drops down to the river and follows the valley bottom.

8. Pass under River Dr. Take time to look at the burned-out ruins of an old paper mill. Built in 1854 by 4 brothers, it produced fine rag paper until John R. Barber, the son of one of the brothers, converted it into a pulp mill. In 1888, John Barber installed a dynamo, and it's thought to be the first electrical generator in Canada that supplied industrial-strength power. You'll see the ruins of the building that housed the dynamo when you've gone another 3k down the trail.

9. Pick up the path as it climbs the hill. The trail seems to fork before it climbs. Take the left fork as it switchbacks up this steep slope.

*The Credit River was so named because the Mississaugas
bought supplies on "credit" before heading out to purchase furs.*

10. The trail skirts the river, which is seldom far from view. A group of canoeists passed by me, and it looked like a fun trip on a warm, clear evening.

11. When you come to a trestle bridge that is high overhead, climb up and pass under it near the top, as the trail now skirts the valley ridge again. Did I mention this is an up-and-down trail?

12. If you walk along here in spring, look for early-season flowers. There were hundreds of trout lilies, trilliums and bloodroot when I walked it in April.

13. The trail drops down again, and at one point, the well-worn path veers right, whereas your blue blazes are to your left. Follow the blazes. Ahead and to your right is a nice opening overlooking the river. Then the trail continues to the ruins of the dynamo building. This is the end of the CVF.

*It doesn't get much better than exploring the Credit River by canoe.*

14. Turn around, retracing your footsteps back to 20th Sideroad/Prince St. near the cemetery. Turn left here and follow the road down into Glen Williams. There are several restaurants in the village as well as lots to look at.

15. At the stop sign, you have a choice of going straight ahead and visiting the Williams Mill Visual Arts Centre. Or you can head into the Copper Kettle Pub. Or maybe turn right and slide into Kit's Little Kitchen for coffee, tea and lunch. Glen Williams has "Weekend Visit" written all over it.

16. When it's time to continue walking, head out of town on Main St. with Kit's Little Kitchen on your left.

17. You pass by 2 churches. I especially like the stone St. Alban the Martyr Anglican Church. Further down the road, you come to Beaumont Mill Antiques & Collectibles, and Kids & Classics Boatshops Museum. With all of the things to do, allow yourself enough time to explore this picturesque village.

18. Continue following Main St. out of the village. From Beaumont Mill Antiques, it's about 1k back to your car. Take care along here as the shoulder is narrow and the sightlines for cars are limited in spots.

# Donovan Bailey/ Bronte Village Loop

## Nicola's
## Insider Info

**LENGTH**
8.4 kilometres

**LEVEL OF DIFFICULTY**
Easy

**LENGTH OF TIME**
2 to 3 hours

**NUMBER OF STEPS**
11,513

**kCAL BURNED** 344

**HIGHLIGHTS**
Yacht club, flowers, weddings, urban/rural combo, waterfront, Bronte Village

**PLACES TO EAT/DRINK**
At The Flavour Fox, the sweet & savoury peanut butter gelato cake caught my fancy. Also try the Sweet! Bakery & Tea House and Taste of Colombia — in Bronte Village just for starters!

**ENTRANCE FEE**
n/a

**TRAILHEAD**
N43° 24.052′ W79° 42.404′

GPS

## TRAIL MARKER
### Loop 9

## OVERVIEW

Like its namesake Donovan Bailey, this route has many golden moments, including Bronte Village and its well-developed waterfront. For those of you thinking, who the heck is Donovan Bailey? Bailey is a Jamaican-born, Canadian sprinter who went to high school in Oakville. He won gold in the 100m sprint in the 1996 Olympic Games in Atlanta. With a time of 9.84 seconds, he held the world record for 3 years. He was billed as "the world's fastest man" after beating Michael Johnson in a 150m competition in Toronto. Bailey won in 14.99 seconds and took home the $1.5-million prize.

Despite this trail's speedy namesake, it's a relaxing route. For local residents, it offers a way to wind down after a hard day at work. You'll find a marina, the lakefront, mansions, coffee shops, pubs, a lovely trail and, the day I was there, weddings, weddings and more weddings. After leaving the Donovan Bailey Trail, you head to the lakeshore, following a network of paths that keeps you almost entirely off streets. You end up near the marina and hundreds of yachts, before arriving in Bronte Village. Then it's down to the waterfront, past all the brides, for a relaxing stroll with gulls and sailboats alongside Lake Ontario.

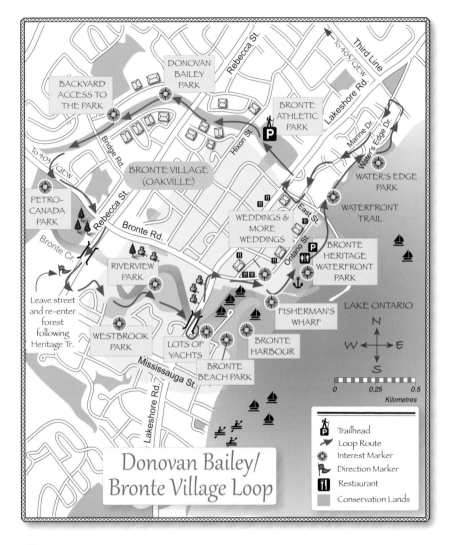

Donovan Bailey/
Bronte Village Loop

# Directions

1. Park in the Bronte Athletic Park (2197 Lakeshore Rd W. in Oakville) with the baseball diamond on your right.

2. The Donovan Bailey Tr. begins at the far end of the parking lot.

3. Stay on this very pleasant, flat and wide trail that connects some fortunate homeowners to an extensive recreational network. This trail follows a corridor once intended to be a road.

4.  Cross Hixon St., Rebecca St. and Bridge Rd., following the Donovan Bailey Park signs.

5.  After crossing Bridge Rd., veer left when you come to a fork in the path.

6.  The trail comes to Bronte Rd. Cross it, being very careful as there are no traffic lights, and then head toward the lake on Bronte Rd.

7.  Follow Bronte Rd. until you come to Rebecca St., where you turn right at the traffic lights.

*Walking the Donovan Bailey Trail is a great way to unwind.*

8.  Follow Rebecca St. over the bridge with Bronte Creek below. Take in the bird's-eye view of the river, noting the flowers blooming along the banks (at least in spring).

9.  Continue walking along Rebecca St., which is the route of the Heritage Tr.

*Ever-present Canada geese.*

10. After another 300m, turn left at the Heritage Tr. sign, leaving Rebecca St. and entering the forest. Turn left at the T-intersection of trails, keeping Bronte Creek on your left. Look for the umbrella-like leaves of mayapples. The scientific name for this plant is a tongue-twisting *Podophyllum peltatum.*

*There is great wedding ogling . . .*

It contains a compound called podophyllin, which is believed to interfere with cell division, and has been considered as a means of treating cancer.

11. Enter Riverview Park and veer right at the Y-intersection of trails. This is Bronte Marsh. At the next intersection of trails, go right. I saw swans and fishermen and people just relaxing in the sunshine here.

12. Go under the overpass for Lakeshore Rd. The trail then goes up an incline to the right. Keep going right until you are on Lakeshore Rd. Cross over the bridge with Bronte Creek below you. This is a great spot to take in the sights and sounds of the yachting world. Listen to omnipresent gulls and rigging clanging against masts.

13. Just after the bridge, continue following Lakeshore Rd. until you come to Bronte Rd. Turn right onto Bronte Rd. Now you're in the heart of Bronte Village, where there are great restaurants, bars, cafés and the like.

*. . . and great backyard ogling on this route!*

*Oakville is home to a lot of yachts.*

14. Continue toward the waterfront. Take the path at the Fisherman's Wharf
    sign to the water's edge. You are in Bronte Heritage Waterfront Park.
    This is a great people-watching place, and we saw 3 colourful weddings
    in progress.

15. Look for the small lighthouse. Before you get to the lighthouse, turn left
    onto the William (Bill) Hill Promenade.

16. Take this lovely waterfront path (part of the Waterfront Tr.) with Lake
    Ontario on your right for 1.5k. Where it ends, turn left onto the short path
    to Water's Edge Dr. and follow it to Third Line. Turn left onto Third Line
    and then left again onto Marine Dr.

17. Follow Marine Dr. for less than 1k to East St.

18. Turn right onto East St., cross Lakeshore Rd. at the traffic lights and then
    turn right, following Lakeshore Rd. for about 100m until you come to your
    car at the Bronte Athletic Park.

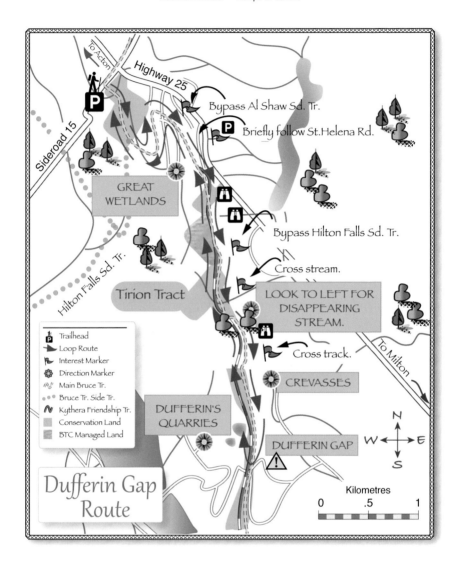

To Acton

Highway 25

To Action

Sideroad 15

P

Bypass Al Shaw Sd. Tr.

P

Briefly follow St. Helena Rd.

GREAT
WETLANDS

Bypass Hilton Falls Sd. Tr.

Cross stream.

Hilton Falls Sd. Tr.

Tirion Tract

LOOK TO LEFT FOR
DISAPPEARING
STREAM.

To Milton

Cross track.

Trailhead
Loop Route
Interest Marker
Direction Marker
Main Bruce Tr.
Bruce Tr. Side Tr.
Kythera Friendship Tr.
Conservation Land
BTC Managed Land

CREVASSES

DUFFERIN'S
QUARRIES

N
W  E
S

DUFFERIN GAP

Dufferin Gap
Route

Kilometres
0      .5      1

"Walk. Breathe. Rejuvenate in nature.
It's a gift to my body, mind and soul"

JEAN SZMIDT

# Dufferin Gap Route
## (Campbellville/Speyside)

*This is an in-and-out route.*

## OVERVIEW

This route replaces the Hilton Falls/Dufferin Gap Loop in the first edition of *Halton Hikes*. One section of that 22.6k loop is no longer open so I had to make a change. This is an in-and-out route. It's beautiful, passing through a plethora of wetlands for the first 2.5k and then following a ridge with an open view to the southeast for the remaining 4.5k.

I suggest everyone who hikes the Bruce Trail should do this hike because it takes you to the Dufferin Gap — the only break in the entire 725k-long, 450-million-year-old Niagara Escarpment. The 40m-long gap, now spanned by a bridge, was allegedly blasted out by an aggregate company to make it quicker for dump trucks to get to Hwy. 401. Built in 1991, the bridge's construction was funded by a combination of corporate, private and public funds. The Dufferin Gap is a horrible sight. You'll be stunned by the contrast to the surrounding landscape. It really is awful to see and to realize how little care some people have for the integrity of our environment, and the plants and animals who live there. Hiking to the Dufferin Gap is an important reminder — and a good route.

**10**

Nicola's
## Insider Info

**LENGTH**
14 kilometres
(9k option)

**LEVEL OF DIFFICULTY**
Challenging

**LENGTH OF TIME**
3.5 to 5 hours
(2.25 to 3 hours)

**NUMBER OF STEPS**
19,099

**kCAL BURNED** 628

**HIGHLIGHTS**
Dufferin Gap,
wetlands, views

**PLACES TO EAT/DRINK**
Milton is pub heaven with
Keenan's Irish Pub, Ivy
Arms, Bryden's Pub and
Ned Devine's Irish Pub

**ENTRANCE FEE** n/a

**TRAILHEAD**
N43° 34.678′W79° 58.619′

**NOTE:** For a shorter
(9k) route park at
N43° 34.251′W79° 57.779′
on St. Helena Rd.

**BRUCE TRAIL MAP** 12

TRAIL MARKER
Loop 10

# Directions

*For the shorter (9k) route from St. Helena Rd. start at Point #10 below.*

1. Park in the Bruce Trail's Pear Tree parking lot on the south side of 15th Sideroad, about 300m west of Hwy. 25. It's between Milton and Acton.

2. For this entire route you will follow the white blazes of the main Bruce Trail, which makes it straightforward, though it's easy to mistakenly head off along some well-used unmarked trails. So, stay alert and keep your eye out for those white blazes.

3. Head south, away from 15th Sideroad, through a garden of donor plaques.

4. When I was there, a few plaques were missing. I later learned that, a while ago, someone came by and stole them, which would be hard to do. Presumably, the thieves thought they were made of brass. But the joke was on the mischief makers since the metal used to make the plaques is worth less than 80 cents a pound!

5. You are walking through the Speyside Resource Management Area.

6. Cross a small bridge by a beautiful pond. Upon entering a cedar forest look back to your left for the remains of a lime kiln. You can see the cut stone, now green with moss and lichens. Limestone rocks were basically melted in these wood-burning ovens to produce the lime used to "chink" log homes.

*The tundra swans seen here have black beaks,*
*whereas trumpeter swans have orange ones.*

7. Bypass the Al Shaw Side Tr., staying on the main Bruce Tr. with its white blazes as it winds its way through a multitude of wetlands. Look for waterfowl and aquatic animals in this rich area.

8. The trail is very rocky so be vigilant to prevent twisting an ankle.

9. Cross another small bridge and note the huge wetland to your right.

10. When you arrive at St. Helena Rd., turn right and follow it to its end. The main Bruce Tr. continues passing by a "Road Closed" sign and concrete barriers. This is the start of the shorter (9k) route.

*It's hard to say what happened here.*

11. This is also the start of the Kythera Hiking – Bruce Trail Friendship Tr. It's one of 9 international friendship trails that have joined up with the Bruce Tr. to celebrate this great form of exercise. Kythera is an area in Greece.

12. While the trail remains rocky, it's less so. Also, it follows a ridge with open views to the southeast. A few paths cross the trail, but continue along the white-blazed main Bruce Tr.

13. You may want to find a sunny spot along this long stretch of trail for a snack or lunch break and to enjoy the view.

*Big foot seems to be fossilized while this rock sported a well-trimmed hairdo.*

*This tragic gap is the only human-made break*
*along the entire length of the Niagara Escarpment.*

*A bridge now spans the Dufferin Gap.*

14. Cross another bridge and a short 20m later look for a faint user-made trail to your right, Follow it for a few metres to where part of the stream flows into a metre-wide hole beneath a tree. The water disappears here, presumably making its way down the escarpment.

15. Large crevices open up on your left as the trail continues to skirt the ridge top. As you near the Dufferin Gap you will begin hearing the large machinery. In contrast, a large, manicured golf course appears to your left.

16. When you arrive at the Dufferin Gap, you'll know it. It's spanned by a 40m-long bridge. To your right are huge machines and industrial buildings. Truck traffic varies but not by much. It's a continuous stream of great belching vehicles amid clouds of dust accompanied by the pounding of excavators.

17. According to the Ontario Stone, Sand & Gravel Association, we use 164-million tonnes of aggregate per year in Ontario, equal to 12 tonnes per person. Some 60% of it is used in "infrastructure," largely roads.

18. This is the turn-around point of the hike. I suggest making a quick getaway until you are out of hearing range of the pits.

19. Follow the same route back to the Pear Tree parking lot continuing to be vigilant to stay on the white-blazed trail and to not twist an ankle on the rocky footing.

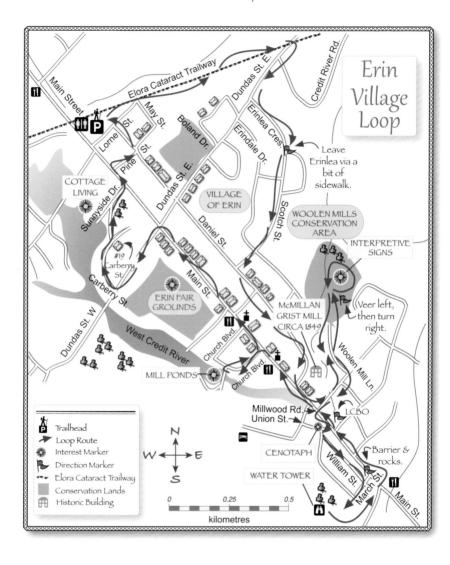

## Erin Village Loop

Leave Erinlea via a bit of sidewalk.

WOOLEN MILLS CONSERVATION AREA

INTERPRETIVE SIGNS

Veer left, then turn right.

COTTAGE LIVING

VILLAGE OF ERIN

#19 Carberry St.

ERIN FAIR GROUNDS

McMILLAN GRIST MILL CIRCA 1849

MILL PONDS

West Credit River

Millwood Rd.
Union St.

LCBO

Barrier & rocks.

CENOTAPH

WATER TOWER

Trailhead
Loop Route
Interest Marker
Direction Marker
Elora Cataract Trailway
Conservation Lands
Historic Building

N
W ← → E
S

0    0.25    0.5
kilometres

*"A hike is cheaper and more effective than any psychologist, and you also get a workout. So cancel the gym membership, cancel the couch session and take the dog."*

DAVID DONALDSON

# Erin Village Loop

## OVERVIEW

I've lived in or near Erin for most of my life, yet it was on this hike that I came across the Woolen Mills Conservation Area for the first time. It's a tiny little park tucked into the banks of the West Credit River with masses of information on interpretive signs. My favourite shows an 1870s photo of Erin with nary a tree, beside a current picture with trees galore — proof that they really had cut down virtually all of the trees by the late 19th century, mostly to supply urban areas with cordwood.

There is a lot to see on this village tour, beginning with a walk along a trail that was once part of the Credit Valley Railway, which connected the village of Cataract to Elora, some 40k apart. You walk by old and new homes, and down the village's main street, where there are plenty of restaurants and shops to add a different sort of sightseeing experience. The trail climbs up to the local water tower, where you get a bird's-eye view of this village of about 4,000 residents. If you're interested, you can download a copy of *A Brief History of Erin Village* by Steve Revell from http://porcupinesquill. ca/images/catalogues/Erin_History.pdf

> *For a café latte and other delicious fare, stop in at the Tin Roof Café. (www.tinroofcafe.ca)*

**11**

### Nicola's
# Insider Info

**LENGTH**
7.8 kilometres

**LEVEL OF DIFFICULTY**
Easy

**LENGTH OF TIME**
2 to 2.5 hours

**NUMBER OF STEPS**
10,765

**kCAL BURNED**  328

**HIGHLIGHTS**
Old mill & flume, Main Street shops, millponds

**PLACES TO EAT/DRINK**
Tin Roof Café has fab lattes and the ginger molasses cookies are my fav. Maddie Hatter Tea Shop & Café offers high tea. Bistro DuPain is croissant heaven. At Holtom's Bakery, try the bath buns.

**ENTRANCE FEE**
n/a

**TRAILHEAD**
N43° 46.741' W80° 04.393'

**GPS**

## TRAIL MARKER
### Loop 11

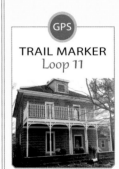

*McMillan's gristmill.*

# Directions

1. Park in the lot for the Elora Cataract Trailway. To get to it, turn east from Main St. onto Ross St. near the north end of the village.

2. Begin walking east along the Trailway so that you're walking away from Main St.

3. Follow this wide, flat trail for about 800m until you come to a road crossing. Turn right here onto Dundas St. E.

4. Follow Dundas St. E for a short 300m and then turn left onto Erinlea Cres.

5. Erinlea Cres. swings left, but you veer right to use a short piece of sidewalk that connects to Scotch St.

6. Follow Scotch St. until you come to Daniel St., where you turn left.

7. Follow Daniel St. for a few blocks until you come to East Church St. where you turn right.

8. When East Church St. hits Main St., turn left and walk through "downtown" Erin.

9. Turn left onto Millwood Rd. Then go left again on Woolen Mill Lane until you come to the Woolen Mills Conservation Area.

10. Enter the conservation area and walk until you come to a fork in the trail. Veer left, following the blue markers.

11. Turn right at the interpretive signs about the old mill and flume, following the blue markers. Reading the interpretive signs as you go, continue on a short circular route that brings you back to these interpretive signs. I was delighted to find this precious conservation area. I just stumbled across it, and I found the photos and other interpretive info really interesting.

12. Leave the conservation area, following Woolen Mill Lane to Millwood Rd., where you turn right.

13. At Main St., turn left, pass the LCBO and cross the street with care.

14. Look for a cenotaph near the spot where the West Credit River passes under the street.

15. Turn right onto Union St. and then left onto William St.

16. Walk along William St., pass by the barrier at the end of the road and then go by a few large rocks. After the rocks, turn right by a shamrock sign and head uphill along a dirt road into a red pine, reforested area on a road that takes you up to the water tower. There is a nice view of the village and beyond from this lofty height (foliage allowing).

17. Don't be tempted to continue walking along the ridge as this is private property. Instead, retrace your steps to the bottom of the hill.

18. Turn right onto an extension of William St. and follow it to a T-intersection.

19. Turn left onto March St. (no street sign) and then left again onto Main St. You may want to stop for a snack or latte in the aptly named Tin Roof Café.

20. Walk along Main St., back into the centre of the village and maybe indulge yourself at Holtom's Bakery or with high tea at the Maddie Hatter Tea Shop & Café.

21. Continue along Main St. until you come to Church Blvd., where there are banks on 2 corners and a set of traffic lights.

22. Turn left and follow Church Blvd. for a short 250m, until you come to Erin's lovely millponds. Water stored in these ponds provided the power needed by Erin's woollen, grist, planing and other mills.

*The Tin Roof Café, a great spot for a latte.*

*Erin's millponds were once turned into great skating rinks in winter.*

Today, they are home to waterfowl. One day as I walked near here, I saw a parade of baby turtles each about the size of a loonie crossing the road. We tried to herd as many as we could so cars wouldn't squish them.

23. Return to Main St. by the same route. Turn left and continue along Main St.

24. You pass by the gates to the Erin Fall Fair, which runs for 4 days every year on the Thanksgiving weekend. This is my favourite fall fair, and 2019 marked its 169th anniversary. The heavy horse pull tops my list of events, but I love looking at all the entries in classes such as Best Peanut Butter Sandwich and Best Tomatoes; a friend of mine always wins the red ribbon for her date squares. The quilts are amazing, and the 1,000lb pumpkins astounding. Referred to as "Ontario's Preview to the Royal [Winter Fair]," it's well worth a visit.

25. Continue along Main St. to Dundas St. W, where you turn left.

26. Just down Dundas St., you come to a lovely and well-cared-for house at #6. This may be what is called a "catalogue house." People could order these houses from the catalogue. The building materials arrived by train.

27. Follow Dundas St. to Carberry St. and turn right.

28. Just ahead, look for a one-way street across from #19 Carberry St. Turn left here onto Sunnyside Dr. (no sign).

29. Follow Sunnyside Dr., past little cottages that back onto the millpond, until it meets Main St.

30. Turn left onto Main St. then right onto Pine St. and follow it to Daniel St.

31. Turn left onto Daniel St. and follow it back to your car.

# Erin Village/ Stanley Park Loop

## Nicola's
## Insider Info

**LENGTH**
9.5 kilometres

**LEVEL OF DIFFICULTY**
Easy

**LENGTH OF TIME**
2.5 to 3.5 hours

**NUMBER OF STEPS**
13,174

**kCAL BURNED** 477

**HIGHLIGHTS**
Main Street shops, canopied 8th Line, cedars on rail trail

**PLACES TO EAT/DRINK**
Bistro DuPain is an amazing French bakery at the north end of Erin. The Tin Roof Café has the best lattes and ginger molasses cookies. Holtom's Bakery is renowned for their doughnuts. I like their white brick loaf. Yum.

**ENTRANCE FEE** n/a

**TRAILHEAD**
N43° 46.741' W80° 04.393'

**TRAIL MARKER**
*Loop 12*

## OVERVIEW

You begin this, the second of 2 wonderful loops in the village of Erin, by walking through Stanley Park. It may not be Vancouver's massive park, but I'd bet money that you'll be surprised at how lovely it is. I'd also take odds that many Erin residents have not ventured through the iconic archway that marks the entrance. People will be pleasantly surprised to see the expansive millponds, where dozens of gulls looked as if they were walking on water when I was there to record this route. (There was a thin layer of ice.) These ponds once offered great skating.

You walk down Main Street where you can stop for "provisions" to take along on your hike, or decide where you'll visit afterwards. There are lots of places to choose from, so I won't pick a favourite — but consider giving Holtom's Bakery a try. Date turnovers anyone? Oatsy Doatsys? The route takes you behind the village, along the quiet and canopied 8th Line. It may be a road, but it's lovely and quiet. Eventually, you arrive at the Elora Cataract Trailway and pass by a magnificent natural cedar hedge.

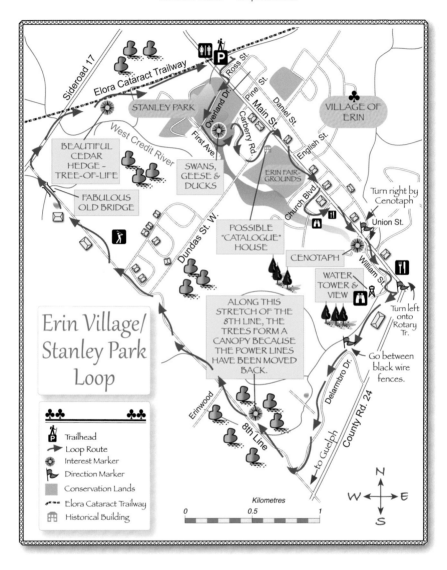

**Erin Village/ Stanley Park Loop**

*Legend:*
- ♣♣♣ Trailhead
- **P** Trailhead
- Loop Route
- Interest Marker
- Direction Marker
- Conservation Lands
- Elora Cataract Trailway
- Historical Building

Map labels:
- Sideroad 17
- Elora Cataract Trailway
- STANLEY PARK
- West Credit River
- BEAUTIFUL CEDAR HEDGE – TREE-OF-LIFE
- FABULOUS OLD BRIDGE
- First Ave.
- Overland Dr.
- Ross St.
- Pine St.
- Carberry Rd.
- Main St.
- Daniel St.
- English St.
- VILLAGE OF ERIN
- SWANS, GEESE & DUCKS
- ERIN FAIR-GROUNDS
- Church Blvd.
- Dundas St. W.
- POSSIBLE "CATALOGUE" HOUSE
- Turn right by Cenotaph
- Union St.
- CENOTAPH
- William St.
- WATER TOWER & VIEW
- ALONG THIS STRETCH OF THE 8TH LINE, THE TREES FORM A CANOPY BECAUSE THE POWER LINES HAVE BEEN MOVED BACK.
- Turn left onto Rotary Tr.
- Go between black wire fences.
- Erinwood
- 8th Line
- Delambro Dr.
- to Guelph
- County Rd. 24

Kilometres
0    0.5    1

N W E S

*"I don't actually hike. But occasionally, when I was younger, the canoe over my head took a wrong, long turn. I still feel, somehow, that a hike is just a long portage where you forgot the canoe. However, I expect it's peaceful. If I were going to hike, that would be why."*

BRUCE MADOLE

*Take a Book/Leave a Book.*

# Directions

1. Park in the lot designated for the Elora Cataract Trailway. To get to it, turn east off Main St. onto Ross St. (no relation) near the north end of the village of Erin.

2. Leave the parking lot by walking along Ross St. to Main St. Cross Main St., with care, and turn left, following it for about 50m.

3. Turn right under the archway that marks the entrance to Stanley Park. But before you do, notice the little "lending library." Someone has attached a lovely cabinet with books inside to a tree. You are invited to "Take a Book/Leave a Book." I didn't partake since I had nowhere to carry one, but there were some excellent books to choose from. I'll go back.

4. Follow the paved road into Stanley Park and get ready to be surprised. On both sides of the road, there are lovely millponds with geese and ducks and gulls and swans whiling away peaceful hours. You won't believe you're mere metres from Erin's main street.

5. Stanley Park was created as a private amusement park that was a popular day trip for Torontonians. It continues to be privately owned today, so please stay on the route I describe and respect homeowners' property.

6. At the intersection of Overland Dr. and First Ave., turn left onto First Ave. Before turning, look ahead and to your right for an old water fountain that's at the edge of a well-manicured forest.

7. When you come to #2 First Ave., turn left and go past a sign that says "No Motorized Vehicles." You're on a causeway between the millponds.

8. The trail comes out to a small grassy parkette; cross it and turn right onto the paved subdivision road (Carberry St.).

9. When you come to a T-intersection, turn left and follow Dundas St. W.

*Millpond in Stanley Park.*

10. Look on your right for #6 Dundas St. W. This neat and tidy, square home, built from stone-like bricks, may be a "catalogue" house: one you purchased from a catalogue. The forms for the bricks came by train. You supplied the concrete.

11. At Main St., turn right and walk toward the village.

12. Turn right onto Church Blvd. at the traffic lights. When the road swings to the left, take a short trip to the bridge, with the millponds to the right and the river below. Then return to Church Blvd. and pick up the Erin Rotary River Tr. at little Riverside Park. Follow this path with the West Credit River to your right. It ends in the Valu-Mart parking lot.

13. Walk through the parking lot and turn right onto Main St. Pick up a few treats or stop for a snack. There's a good ice cream shop nearer the south end of the village.

14. Turn right onto Charles St. for a short in-and-out to view the river again.

15. At Union St. where there's a cenotaph, turn right and follow Union St. as it turns left and becomes William St.

16. At the end of William St., go past the barricade and pass by a few large rocks. Look for a shamrock sign on your right. Turn right past it and head uphill along a dirt road into a red pine, reforested area.

17. Part way up the hill, turn left onto the Rotary Tr. (If you want a view of Erin, continue up the road to the water tower and return.)

18. Stay on the steps as the Rotary Tr. goes down an incline. DO NOT take the trail that goes straight ahead. Follow the Rotary

*Christmas in what looks like summer.*

Tr. into a cedar bush and then behind an apartment building.

19. After 200m, the Rotary Tr. ends. Pass between 2 black wire fences into a subdivision. Turn right and follow Delambro Dr. through the subdivision.

20. When you come to a T-intersection, turn right onto 8th Line. This is a quiet, really pretty dirt road. Along one section, the hydro poles are behind the trees. As a result, the large maples have formed a fabulous canopy that provides some shade on a hot day.

21. Follow 8th Line through a marshy area, around 2 sharp bends and up a steep hill. At the top of the hill, turn left at the T-intersection, continuing to follow 8th Line.

22. The road drops down past a golf course and gives you a lovely view of the surrounding landscape. You cross the West Credit River, over an old and pretty concrete bridge.

23. When you come to another T-intersection, turn right and follow 17th Sideroad. It's a busy road, but you're only on it for 400m.

24. When you come to the Elora Cataract Trailway, turn right onto the Trailway.

25. Stop at the interpretive sign that describes the magnificent natural hedge of Eastern white cedars that lines this stretch of trail. Cedars are referred to as the "tree of life," because a tea made from them has been used to cure scurvy because it contains vitamin C.

26. Follow the Trailway and cross Wellington Road 124 (Main St.) carefully, as it's busy. Stay on the Trailway until you return to the parking lot and your car.

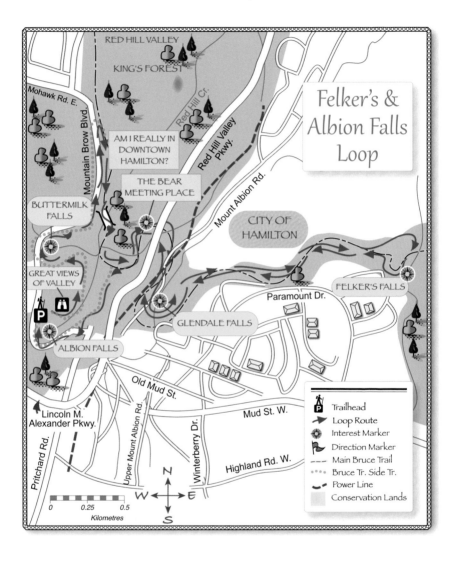

## Felker's & Albion Falls Loop

RED HILL VALLEY

KING'S FOREST

Mohawk Rd. E.

Mountain Brow Blvd.

Red Hill Ct.

Red Hill Valley Pkwy.

AM I REALLY IN DOWNTOWN HAMILTON?

THE BEAR MEETING PLACE

Mount Albion Rd.

CITY OF HAMILTON

BUTTERMILK FALLS

GREAT VIEWS OF VALLEY

FELKER'S FALLS

Paramount Dr.

GLENDALE FALLS

ALBION FALLS

Old Mud St.

Lincoln M. Alexander Pkwy.

Pritchard Rd.

Upper Mount Albion Rd.

Winterberry Dr.

Mud St. W.

Highland Rd. W.

N
W — E
S

0    0.25    0.5
Kilometres

**Legend**
- Trailhead
- Loop Route
- Interest Marker
- Direction Marker
- Main Bruce Trail
- Bruce Tr. Side Tr.
- Power Line
- Conservation Lands

*"I hike to clear my mind, to lessen the deafening buzz of society and to reunite myself with the earth. I hike to feel the breeze on my skin and receive whispers rippling in the streams from the universe's internal energy. I hike to rediscover the land and myself. I hike to escape and be found. I hike because I can."*

PAULA BILZ

# Felker's & Albion Falls Loop (Hamilton)

## OVERVIEW

I kept hearing about Hamilton's waterfalls, so I decided to explore. While Hamilton isn't in Halton Region, I included this loop to whet your appetite for my Hamilton & Area guide. It features many of this area's more than 100 cascades. Two of four waterfalls (Felker's and Albion) that you see on this loop are included in Day Trips Canada's list of Southwestern Ontario's 10 best.

The waterfalls are the highlight, but the entire route is great. I saw lots of birds, including colourful Baltimore orioles and elegant Northern flickers, and despite being within the City of Hamilton, you are almost entirely on forested trails. The walk along the mountain brow provides stunning views of the enormous Red Hill Valley, as well as of Hamilton and Lake Ontario. This route really shows off Ontario's 5th largest city. If the Red Hill Valley sounds familiar, it's because the 7k Red Hill Valley Pkwy. runs through it. This expressway connects the Lincoln M. Alexander Pkwy. to the 403/QEW. The former opened in 2007 despite decades of opposition that included a long occupation by those who argued that building the highway would undermine efforts to combat climate change.

## Nicola's Insider Info

**LENGTH**
10 kilometres

**LEVEL OF DIFFICULTY**
Moderate

**LENGTH OF TIME**
2.5 to 3.5 hours

**NUMBER OF STEPS**
13,650

**kCAL BURNED** 419

**HIGHLIGHTS**
Waterfalls, mountain-brow walk

**PLACES TO EAT/DRINK**
According to TripAdvisor, the following are Hamilton's best coffee shops: The Cannon, Detour Café, Jitterbug Café, Mulberry Street Coffee House and Saint James Espresso Bar. We have soft spots for the Paisley Coffeehouse & Eatery and Durand Coffee.

**ENTRANCE FEE** n/a

**TRAILHEAD**
N43° 12.304′ W79° 49.150′

**BRUCE TRAIL MAP** 7

GPS

**TRAIL MARKER**
Loop 13

# Directions

1. The parking lot is tricky to find so you may want to google the trailhead GPS coordinates found in Nicola's Insider Info. You are looking for the Albion Falls Observation Platform parking lot in The Upper King's Forest in Hamilton. You access it from Mountain Brow Blvd.

2. Leave your car and head toward the Albion Mill millstone and lookout. This is 1 of 2 lookouts with a view of beautiful Albion Falls.

3. After snapping a few photos, go left (away from the falls) following the blue blazes of the Mountain Brow Side Tr. The large Red Hill Valley is on your right. Follow this lovely trail, taking in the vistas.

4. About 1k later, you come to a road. Before turning onto it, take a look at the 2nd waterfall for the day. This is Buttermilk Falls. Smaller, but lovely.

5. Turn right onto the road, cross the bridge over a creek and then turn right at the end of the bridge and head back into the forest. This is all marked with the blue blazes of a Bruce Tr. side trail.

6. The next stretch of trail provides views of Hamilton and Lake Ontario.

*Red Hill Creek.*

*Walk this loop to see which waterfall this is.*

7. The trail comes back onto the road before you arrive at the Red Hill Creek Side Tr. Turn right onto the Red Hill Creek Side Tr. and head down the stairs, still following blue blazes.

8. Partway down into the valley, you meet the main Bruce Tr. with its white blazes. The Red Hill Creek Side Tr. ends here, as do the blue blazes. Keep going straight ahead following the white blazes of the main Bruce Tr.

9. At the valley bottom, cross a pedestrian bridge and then go right.

10. You come to a spot where the Bruce Tr. blazes are a bit confusing. One shows a blue side trail turning right, and the other shows a white blaze that seems to go straight. Go straight up the little rise, ignoring the blue blazes. At the top of the little rise, keep going straight, following the white blazes. DO NOT follow the Mountain Brow Side Tr. and its blue blazes. The main Bruce Tr. makes a sharp left turn and takes you to The Bear Meeting Place where there are interpretive signs. It's a good place for lunch or a snack.

11. Just after The Bear and before a sign about the Red Hill Valley Tr., turn right following the white blazes. This turn is easy to miss, so pay attention.

Red-winged blackbird.

The trail goes past a pond that may be alive with red-winged blackbirds and croaking frogs.

12. Pass under the Red Hill Valley Pkwy. and turn right onto the abandoned Mud St. as it climbs out of the valley.

13. Once you've reached the top, stay alert so you don't miss the main Bruce Tr. on your left. Follow it as it re-enters the forest. Pass by the Kingsview Dr. Side Tr. On your left is a nice stream with your 3rd waterfall: little Glendale Falls.

14. Pass the Paramount Park Side Tr., following white blazes. In about 30 minutes you arrive at Felker's Falls. It is a "terraced ribbon falls" that drops 22m. The Felker family owned this land for 140 years.

15. Just past Felker's Falls, you come to a paved path. There are 2 interesting interpretive signs on your left.

16. At this T-intersection of trails, turn right onto the paved Peter St. Tr. and then go right again, heading back into the forest. Take the left fork, just inside the forest. Follow this trail until it meets the main Bruce Tr. Then veer left and follow the main trail's white blazes.

17. Pass by the Paramount Park and Kingsview Dr. Side trails, go under the parkway and enjoy the pond and The Bear again.

18. When you come to an intersection of trails, you leave the main Bruce Tr. by turning left onto the blue-blazed Mountain Brow Side Tr., where you start climbing.

19. At the next trail intersection, DO NOT take the well-worn Mud Street Side Tr. Instead, veer right, off the cinder path, staying on the smaller Mountain Brow Side Tr.

20. Follow it back to the road. The parking lot and your car are to your right.

# Glen Abbey
## Loop (Oakville)

## OVERVIEW

This great loop will give you a taste of the extensive trail network in this part of Oakville. It's amazing!

If you know the name Glen Abbey, it's likely because the Glen Abbey Golf Club hosted the Canadian Open 30 times — more than any other club. The course was the work of the golf legend: Jack Nicklaus. The golf club's property has an interesting history, which accounts for why so many of the nearby streets have names like Monks Pass and Pilgrim's Way. In the 1930s, Andre Doorman built a large stone home on a 140-hectare estate where he lived with his family. In 1953, the Jesuit Fathers of Upper Canada purchased the property, turning the house into a monastery, and the surrounding property into farmland. Eventually, it was sold again and had several lives as a golf course, eventually becoming the Glen Abbey Golf Club and home to the Royal Canadian Golf Association. Some people may recall that in the early 1970s it was a ski club with a T-bar lift.

This loop is all on trails and not far from some great cafés and restaurants. Hats off to the Town of Oakville for these trails.

**14**

### Nicola's
## Insider Info

LENGTH
6.7 kilometres

LEVEL OF DIFFICULTY
Easy

LENGTH OF TIME
1.5 to 2.5 hours

NUMBER OF STEPS
8,334

kCAL BURNED 267

HIGHLIGHTS
Tulip tree, shagbark hickory, away-from-it-all

PLACES TO EAT/DRINK
Vereda Central Coffee Roasters, Monastery Bakery, Kerr Street Café, Stoney's Bread Co., Taste of Colombia in Oakville

ENTRANCE FEE
n/a

TRAILHEAD
N43° 26.104' W79° 44.290'

GPS

TRAIL MARKER
Loop 14

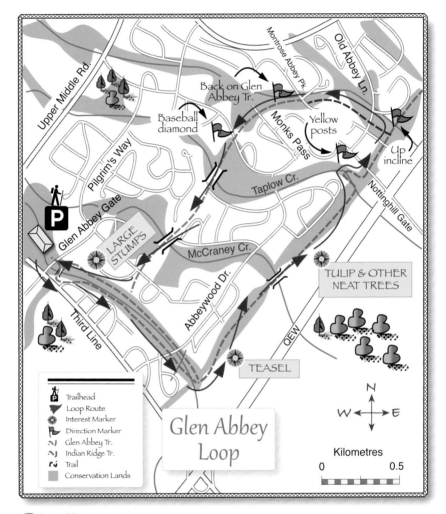

Glen Abbey Loop

Legend:
- Trailhead
- Loop Route
- Interest Marker
- Direction Marker
- Glen Abbey Tr.
- Indian Ridge Tr.
- Trail
- Conservation Lands

## Directions

1. Park at the south end of the Glen Abbey Community Centre parking lot. It's just south of Upper Middle Rd. on Third Line.

2. Cross Glen Abbey Gate, the street that borders the south end of the community centre. On the other side of the road, look for a sign that reads "Glen Abbey Trail" and follow this path that quickly changes from pavement to cinder.

3. Almost immediately (after 50m), turn right at a Y-intersection and cross a bridge over a small creek that feeds into Sixteen Mile Cr.

4. Follow this peaceful trail for 1.25k until the trail ends at Indian Ridge Tr. Along the way, you bypass another path and cross Abbeywood Dr.

5. Turn left onto Indian Ridge Tr. There's a sign here telling you that McCraney Creek Tr. is 820m away.

6. Indian Ridge Tr. has an open view to the south where you can hear

*Some people suggest teasel is semi-carnivorous.*

and see the QEW. I soon tuned out the roar, enjoying this long stretch of seldom-travelled trail. I noticed teasel growing alongside the trail. It looks like a cross between a thistle and a bullrush. It's noteworthy because it's often said to be partially carnivorous. Insects, the theory goes, drown in small water-filled cups around the plant's stem. The plant absorbs nutrients from this water, which helps it grow. Researchers, however, tested this theory and found no evidence that insect-rich water helped teasel in any way.

7. After about 750m, at a trail intersection with a sign noting it's 300m to Potter's Wheel Park, veer right. Cross over a small bridge, staying on Indian Ridge Tr.

8. The Town of Oakville has planted lots of trees along this trail; some are a bit exotic for people like me, who live farther north and at a considerably higher elevation. In particular, look for the indigenous tulip tree (see photo). There are black walnuts and shagbark hickory, too.

9. At the next trail intersection (Taplow Cr.), turn right toward yellow posts, and then right again at the yellow poles.

10. Carefully cross Nottingham Gate, a wide street, and then keep going straight.

11. Note the sign warning of coyotes. If you have a dog, make sure it's on a leash.

*Tulip tree (Liriodendron tulipifera)*

*This section of trail begs you to go for a walk.*

12. At the next trail intersection, veer left heading up an incline into Montrose Abbey Pk. and leaving Indian Ridge Tr.

13. Cross Old Abbey Lane and you will see a sign indicating you are on Glen Abbey Tr. again.

14. At a new bridge, veer left away from the bridge, pass a bench and cross Montrose Abbey Dr., staying on Glen Abbey Tr.

15. Note a beautiful garden below and to your right behind a black metal fence.

16. At the end of the black metal fence, the trail goes sharply left and crosses a road called Monks Passage.

17. Cross Nottingham Gate again and enter Glen Abbey Woods. At the baseball diamond, veer right.

18. At the end of the ball diamond, it's a bit tricky. There is a Y-intersection of trails where you veer left and then turn right. Entering the forest, cross over a small bridge.

19. Stay on Abbey Glen Tr. as you cross Taplow Cr. Tr. and Taplow Cr. Ignore the paths that are connectors to houses.

20. The Glen Abbey Tr. becomes paved. Stay straight at a sign that reads "This Section of Trail adopted by The Strathdee Family." (Thank you, Strathdees!)

21. Cross a small bridge over McCraney Cr. and veer right.

22. Cross Pilgrims Way (a street) and keep going until you come to a T-intersection of trails where there's a wooden fence in front of you.

23. Turn right here. You are on the homestretch.

24. Follow this cinder path, noting the stumps of what were enormous, likely maple trees. I wonder what happened to them.

25. At the next trail intersection, you'll see a bridge to your left. This is the bridge you crossed when you first began this loop. Bypass the bridge, cross Glen Abbey Gate and return to your car.

# Glen Williams
# Village Loop

## OVERVIEW

Glen Williams is a fabulous village, so I was determined to find a loop that passed through it, especially since you can now get a latte at Kit's Little Kitchen! In addition to interesting places to eat, there's the marvellous Williams Mill Visual Arts Centre, where you can see artists in action. The Copper Kettle Pub has the best outdoor patio, and The Glen Tavern is a gem. Further up the road is Beaumont Mill Antiques & Collectibles, which is my kind of antique store, filled as it is with little nooks and crannies overflowing with wonderful items to wonder at and possibly purchase. Next door is The Feathered Nest with architectural treasures. So put some cash in your pocket and shine up them hiking boots.

This loop starts with a forest walk along a trail high on a ridge. It's part of the Credit Valley Footpath and is carved into a steepish slope, so you have some wonderful vistas of the Credit River below when there are no leaves to obstruct your view. Next is the Glen Williams Cemetery, which is worth a visit for a look back in time and for the view.

> Stop by the **Copper Kettle Pub** in *Glen Williams.*
> (**www.copperkettle.ca**) *Fresh Food | Local Brews |*
> *Live Music | Fabulous Patio | Wood-burning Fireplace*

**15**

## Nicola's
## Insider Info

LENGTH
4.6 kilometres

LEVEL OF DIFFICULTY
Easy

LENGTH OF TIME
1 to 1.5 hours

NUMBER OF STEPS
6,877

kCAL BURNED 209

HIGHLIGHTS
Glen Williams Cemetery, Williams Mill Visual Arts Centre

PLACES TO EAT/DRINK
The Glen Tavern is open for dinner with a full and wonderful menu. The Copper Kettle Pub is open for lunch and dinner. I always have the black bean & chickpea burger and a local brew. Kit's Little Kitchen serves up lattes and is known for its Irish scones.

ENTRANCE FEE n/a

TRAILHEAD
N43° 41.100'W79° 55.598'

GPS

TRAIL MARKER
Loop 15

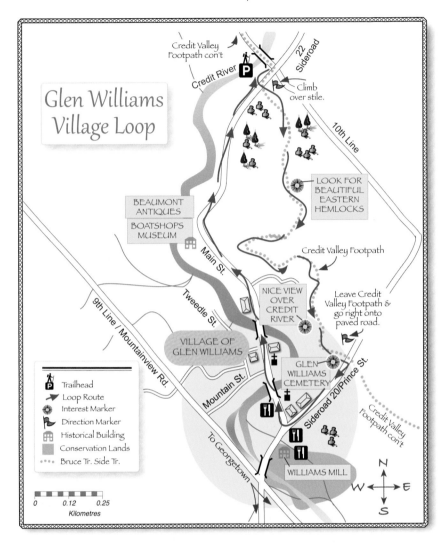

# Glen Williams Village Loop

Credit Valley Footpath con't

Credit River

22 Sideroad

Climb over stile.

10th Line

LOOK FOR BEAUTIFUL EASTERN HEMLOCKS

BEAUMONT ANTIQUES

BOATSHOPS MUSEUM

Main St.

Credit Valley Footpath

Leave Credit Valley Footpath & go right onto paved road.

Tweedle St.

NICE VIEW OVER CREDIT RIVER

9th Line / Mountainview Rd.

VILLAGE OF GLEN WILLIAMS

Mountain St.

GLEN WILLIAMS CEMETERY

Sideroad 20/Prince St.

Credit Valley Footpath con't

To Georgetown

WILLIAMS MILL

N
W — E
S

**Legend:**
- Trailhead
- Loop Route
- Interest Marker
- Direction Marker
- Historical Building
- Conservation Lands
- Bruce Tr. Side Tr.

0    0.12    0.25
Kilometres

*"Hiking. When and where else can you chat with a friend for as many hours as you like without any interruption at all?"*

DON FERGUSON

# Directions

1. Park at the intersection of 22nd Siteroad and 10th Line in Halton Hills, just north of Georgetown. Much of the land in this area is owned by Sheridan Nurseries, so rows of trees and bushes fill the fields. There is no designated parking area, but the shoulder is wide with lots of room for your car.

2. Turn right, heading west on 22nd Siteroad with the hill to your left. Almost immediately, you see a blue Bruce Tr. sign identifying the Credit Valley Footpath (CVF). Climb the stile on the left side of the road and head straight ahead, up the slope on a lane.

*View from the cemetery*

3. In about 100m, follow the well-worn trail as it heads uphill, veers off to the left and crosses a wooden bridge.

4. The trail runs just below the crest of the hill, so you feel a bit as though you are hidden from the world. Look for patches of bloodroot, wild ginger and trilliums in the spring.

5. To your right, there are some nice views of the Credit River below when the trees are bare of leaves.

6. Follow the blue blazes of this Bruce Tr. side trail, also looking for pink, purple and white dame's rocket (similar to phlox), and miniature bamboo-like horsetail ferns (also known as pot-scrubbing ferns). You may also see garlic mustard. I've heard you can make a tasty pesto using the leaves of this invasive species.

7. The trail comes out into the Glen Williams Cemetery with graves dating back to the 1800s. So take some time to explore. From the edge of the cemetery, there's a nice view of the village at your feet.

8. Exit the cemetery through its entrance. You leave the CVF here. Turn right and head downhill on the paved road (20th Siteroad/Prince St.). There are several beautiful old Ontario houses along this winding road.

*St. Alban the Martyr Anglican Church.*

*Kids & Classics Boatshops Museum.*

9. Next is the very explorable village of Glen Williams. You may not make it much past the stop sign, deciding instead to head into the Copper Kettle Pub or the Williams Mill Visual Arts Centre. Or maybe you'll turn right and opt for a latte at Kit's Little Kitchen. Really, this is a village with "Weekend Visit" written all over it.

10. When you decide it's time to continue walking, head out of town on Main St., passing Kit's Little Kitchen on your left. The surrounding homes with their inviting porches and established gardens add to the welcoming feel of the village.

11. Cross the Credit River twice and pass by 2 old churches. I especially like the stone St. Alban the Martyr Anglican Church. Further down the road are Beaumont Mill Antiques & Collectibles, the Kids & Classics Boatshops Museum and The Feathered Nest. With all of these temptations, allow yourself enough time to explore this picturesque village.

12. Follow Main St. out of the village. Take care as the shoulders are narrow and visibility is limited in places. It's about 1k back to your car.

# Great Esker Loop
## (Terra Cotta/Glen Williams)

## OVERVIEW

I walked this route on a glorious November afternoon. Much of the trail follows a ridgetop that overlooks the valley that Silver Creek flows through en route to the Credit River. I scared up a grouse, came across a stand of resplendent tamaracks and my hiking shoes mashed fallen apples that were baking in the warm sunshine. The apples' rich aroma reminded me of being a kid on the farm in Caledon.

This route offers great views from atop the Great Esker. It's situated in a huge expanse of publicly owned land that includes Scotsdale Farm as well as the Silver Creek and Terra Cotta Conservation Areas. Together, they reach from east of Winston Churchill Blvd. to Trafalgar Road.

When I returned to my car, two women were sitting on a rock looking forlorn. I asked them if they were lost. They said no, they were simply tired and were trying to get a taxi to pick them up and take them back to their car — some 18k away. I offered them a lift, which they gladly accepted. I told them I was researching a new hiking guide and they each bought a copy of Caledon Hikes — proof that you will be rewarded for a good deed.

*If you want to enjoy hiking in Halton from your doorstep, contact Jill Johnson at Royal LePage Meadowtowne Realty (905-873-5592). Read about her hiking for charity activities at www.jilljohnson.ca.*

## 16

### Nicola's
## Insider Info

**LENGTH**
8.4 kilometres

**LEVEL OF DIFFICULTY**
Moderate

**LENGTH OF TIME**
2 to 3 hours

**NUMBER OF STEPS**
11,576

**kCAL BURNED** 454

**HIGHLIGHTS**
Views, the esker, tamaracks, white pines

**PLACES TO EAT/DRINK**
In Glen Williams: the Glen Tavern is open for dinner with a full and wonderful menu, The Copper Kettle Pub is open for lunch and dinner. I always have the Black Bean & Chickpea Burger and a local brew. Kit's Little Kitchen serves up lattes and is known for its Irish scones./In Terra Cotta, try the Terra Cotta Inn & Pub (closed Mon./Pub opens at 5pm on weekdays/11:30am on weekends), the Terra Cotta Country Store

**ENTRANCE FEE** n/a

**TRAILHEAD**
N43° 41.528'W79° 58.021'

**BRUCE TRAIL MAP** 13

GPS

## TRAIL MARKER
### Loop 16

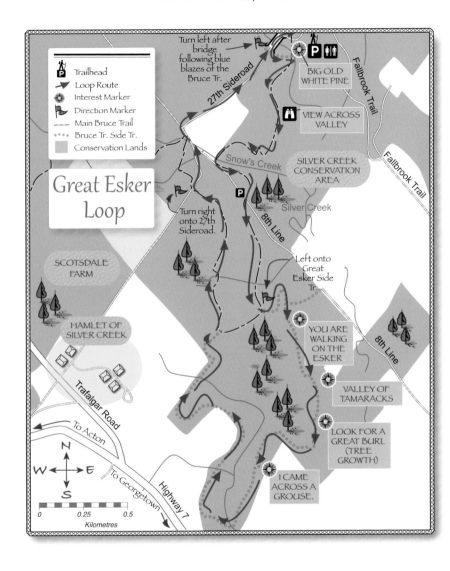

**Great Esker Loop**

Legend:
- **P** Trailhead
- Loop Route
- Interest Marker
- Direction Marker
- Main Bruce Trail
- Bruce Tr. Side Tr.
- Conservation Lands

Turn left after bridge following blue blazes of the Bruce Tr.

27th Sideroad

Fallbrook Trail

BIG OLD WHITE PINE

VIEW ACROSS VALLEY

Snow's Creek

SILVER CREEK CONSERVATION AREA

Silver Creek

8th Line

Turn right onto 27th Sideroad.

Left onto Great Esker Side Tr.

SCOTSDALE FARM

HAMLET OF SILVER CREEK

YOU ARE WALKING ON THE ESKER

8th Line

Trafalgar Road

VALLEY OF TAMARACKS

LOOK FOR A GREAT BURL (TREE GROWTH)

To Acton

N
W — E
S

To Georgetown

Highway 7

I CAME ACROSS A GROUSE.

0    0.25    0.5
Kilometres

*"Being surrounded by the peaceful green is calming;
breathing in air that feels so cool and clean is refreshing;
working my body hard, although tiring, is rejuvenating; listening
to the sounds of the forest connects me with our primal past."*

CAROL SHEPPARD

# Directions

1. Park on Fallbrook Tr. where it abuts 27th Sideroad. This is north and east of Georgetown in Halton Hills, within the boundaries of the Silver Creek Conservation Area. Note that this conservation area has been mostly left in its natural state with few facilities other than a great network of trails. It's a relatively undisturbed environment for flora and fauna. The road has wide shoulders that accommodate parking, and there is a portable washroom.

2. Walk west on 27th Sideroad, with the white barn on your right.

3. You will be on the road for less than 400m and get to cross an interesting bridge over Silver Creek. The bridge has been reconstructed, but they cleverly kept the original stone structure intact.

4. Just after the bridge, turn left, leaving the road and passing through a fence on a trail marked by the blue blazes of a Bruce Tr. side trail. Look to your right. There is an enormous white pine that towers above the other trees.

5. When blue blazes give way to the main Bruce Tr.'s white blazes, veer right following the white blazes.

6. The trail follows the edge of the deep valley where Silver Creek flows. The lofty view along this ridge makes you feel as though you are up in the treetops. You then drop down into the valley and take a bridge over the crystal clear Snow's Creek. Stick with the white-blazed trail as it leads you to the right and up to the 8th Line.

7. Cross 8th Line and pick up the trail directly on the other side. It's near a small parking area. About 600m later, you arrive at the Great Esker Side Tr. Turn left here and follow its blue blazes.

8. Walk up the moderate incline that runs along a ridgetop. This is the esker. For those of you who don't know, an esker is a gravel ridge left behind by a glacier.

*Silver Creek.*

*Autumn's bounty.*

9. Further along, there is a magnificent view over a valley of tamarack trees. In any season except autumn, you would mistake these trees for evergreens, but when I walked by they were brilliantly yellow, reminding me that they are our only deciduous conifers.

10. Cross Silver Creek a few more times before the Great Esker Side Tr. ends at the main Bruce Tr. At this junction, turn left following the white blazes. Keep a lookout for this junction, as it is easy to just wander onto the main Bruce Tr. going in the wrong direction.

11. The trail comes to a paved road (27th Sideroad). Turn right onto it and follow it as it combines with the 8th Line for a few metres before branching off to the right again. There is a working farm on the corner that's an island of privately owned land within this enormous block of public space.

12. Follow 27th Sideroad back over the pretty bridge to Fallbrook Tr. and your car.

*Valley of tamaracks.*

# Guelph Radial Line
## Linear Route (Rockwood/Acton)

*This route can be buggy. It's mostly well-marked with orange blazes. There are stiles that pose a problem for some dogs.*

## OVERVIEW

This linear route comprises the Halton portion of the 33.3k Guelph Radial Line Trail, which connects lovely Eden Mills to charming Limehouse. It requires a car drop and a good chunk of time.

At the time of writing, several sections of this route were closed. Hopefully, the one through the Scout camp (5th Line to the 6th Line in Nassagaweya) will reopen post-Covid. Currently, there is no reasonable way to get around this closure. As a result, you can only walk this route in sections at present (summer 2021). Fortunately, there are some great in-and-out hikes. In order of preference, I suggest: 6th Line Nassagaweya to Dublin Line (~4.5k one way), 2nd Line Nassagaweya to Guelph Line (~1.8k one way), Hwy. 25 to 4th Line Halton (~4k one way).

This route includes magnificent forests with steep slopes as well as the scenic Blue Springs area that is also featured in the Bear Den Loop (page 33). For updates on the Radial Line Trail, visit the Guelph Hiking Trail Club (www.guelphhiking.com). The trail vaguely follows the electric Guelph Radial Line, which operated until 1931 at speeds up to 130kph.

> *Drop by* **Caledon Hills Cycling** *in Inglewood for great gear, fabulous cycling, spectacular hiking, snowshoeing, cross-country skiing and to meet our friendly and well-informed staff.* **(caledonhillscycling.com)**

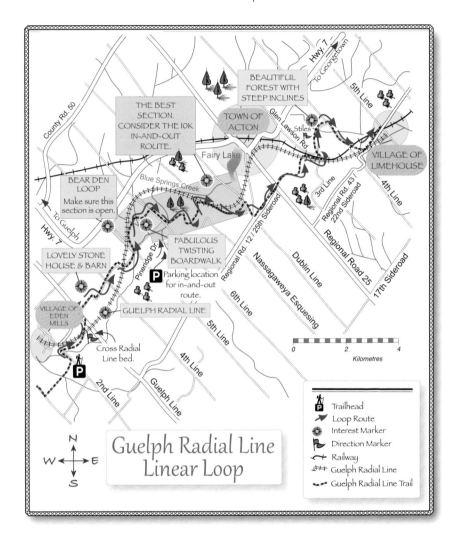

BEAUTIFUL FOREST WITH STEEP INCLINES

THE BEST SECTION. CONSIDER THE 10K IN-AND-OUT ROUTE.

TOWN OF ACTON

VILLAGE OF LIMEHOUSE

BEAR DEN LOOP
Make sure this section is open.

Fairy Lake

Blue Springs Creek

FABULOUS TWISTING BOARDWALK

LOVELY STONE HOUSE & BARN

Parking location for in-and-out route.

VILLAGE OF EDEN MILLS

GUELPH RADIAL LINE

Cross Radial Line bed.

Glen Lawson Rd.

Stiles

County Rd. 50

To Guelph

Hwy. 7

Pineridge Dr.

Regional Rd. 12 / 25th Sideroad

Nassagaweya Esquesing

6th Line

5th Line

4th Line

Guelph Line

2nd Line

3rd Line

22nd Sideroad

Regional Rd. 43 /

Dublin Line

Regional Road 25

17th Sideroad

4th Line

5th Line

Hwy. 7

To Georgetown

0    2    4

Kilometres

**Guelph Radial Line Linear Loop**

N
W — E
S

Trailhead
Loop Route
Interest Marker
Direction Marker
Railway
Guelph Radial Line
Guelph Radial Line Trail

*"Being outside, and particularly in the woods,*
*simply makes me happy. A group of awesome ladies*
*and some delightful lunch = I am happy."*

DIANE MADDEN

# Directions

## Option 1 (24.1k total hike)

1.  Park on 2nd Line in Nassagaweya, 2k northeast of the village of Eden Mills. There is no designated parking, but the road is quiet and there is enough of a shoulder to park safely. The trailhead is by the bridge that spans Blue Springs Creek, just south of 30th Sideroad.

2.  The trail you want heads into the forest going east, just north of the bridge. Make sure you go east and not west.

3.  Both times I hiked this route, it was hot and muggy. I was immediately struck by the treasure trove of wild ginger in the forest (poison ivy, too). I also noted how the temperature dropped by at least 5°C under the tree cover.

4.  For the next 1.8k, you walk in the forest, following the orange blazes of the Guelph Radial Line Tr. (GRLTr.). Near to Guelph Line, you cross the radial rail line, but you won't actually walk along it. In fact, very little of this 24k route follows the old railbed; it mostly skirts around it.

5.  When you arrive at a road, climb the stile and turn left onto busy Guelph Ln. Turn right onto 30th Sideroad. Follow this quiet road past some lovely stone buildings for 3.5k, crossing 4th Line en route to 5th Line.

*This beauty is one of many in this area.*

6. When you arrive at 5th Line, turn left onto it, keeping your eyes open for where the trail re-enters the woods on your right. There is a gate and a little archway that you walk under. (This section was closed due to Covid. Check **www.guelphhiking.com** to see if it has reopened. The only way around is a long walk along roads and I don't recommend it.)

7. For the next 1k you are on the railbed. It's overgrown with cedars that almost form a tunnel, which makes for a different hike. After 1k, you come to a fabulous boardwalk that wends its way through the trees. It's a work of art, with lots of wiggles and rounded edges. I salute those who built this boardwalk.

8. At the end of the boardwalk, turn right, following the orange blazes and some black markers.

9. When you come to a sign and blue blazes for the Blue Springs Side Tr., turn hard left, following the orange blazes. There are also yellow and blue markers on this section of trail. There is a left turn at the bottom of a hill that is easy to miss. If you find yourself looking at a blue sign that says "Archery Range," turn around — you've missed that left-hand turn. (If this section has re-opened, these directions may be out of date. Check **www.guelphhiking.com** for directions. When in doubt, follow the orange blazes, which mark the GRLTr.)

*The old rail line is tunnel-like in places.*

10. When you arrive at a road, turn right and follow what is 6th Line for about 700m. Keep your eyes open for where the trail re-enters the forest on the other (left) side of the road.

11. For the next 300m, the trail parallels the road until the path disappears, and you find yourself back on 6th Line. Keep walking along 6th Line until you come to Pineridge Dr. The trail re-enters the forest to your left directly across from Pineridge Dr.

*After spending time in the forest, this view
of a hummocky moraine was a welcome change.*

12. When I walked this section with a friend, we heard a loon, which was very
    Canadian. For the next 5k, the trail takes you through young and mature
    hardwood forests, and dank cedar woods. You skirt farmers' fields, pass by
    small wetlands and climb a ridge that looks out over a hummocky moraine.
    As I mention in the Overview, I highly recommend doing this section from
    6th Line to Dublin Line as an in-and-out route. You will even walk along the
    old rail line for a short time and cross several rickety bridges over small, clear
    streams. Hiking bliss (see directions for shorter **Option 2** on page 104).

13. Turn right onto Dublin Line and follow it to 22nd Sideroad. Turn left onto
    22 Sideroad until you come
    to busy Halton Rd. 25. Cross
    it with care and continue
    straight ahead into some
    farm fields.

14. You follow the edge of farm
    fields for 750m. Look to your
    left, noticing the raised rail
    bed across the field. When
    the fields end, head back
    into the forest continuing to
    follow the orange blazes.

*I love stone barns,
and this one is in great condition.*

15. The trail passes through a beautiful mature forest and has lots of ups and downs, some of them steep. Walk along a short section of the radial line before going down a slope and arriving at 3rd Line, right by a live set of railway tracks.

16. Turn left onto 3rd Line, cross the railway tracks carefully and continue down the hill on the road. At the bottom, you arrive at Glen Lawson Rd. Turn right onto Glen Lawson Rd. and follow it for less than 500m.

17. Look for a stile on your left. Climb it. For this next section, you really need to follow the orange blazes as there are lots of ATV trails.

18. Climb a 2nd stile, and then arrive at a 3rd, which you can walk around.

19. It's beautiful in this forest, with short, really steep sections. But it's crisscrossed by ATV trails, so beware. Look for some enormous old-growth maple trees.

20. Climb straight up a steep pitch and come out onto 4th Line.

21. Turn right and follow 4th Line to 22 Sideroad. Turn left onto 22 Sideroad and follow it into Limehouse where you will find your car, if you dropped one off.

22. This is the terminus of the GRLTr. and the end of your very long hike. Congrats!

## Option 2 (9k total hike)

1. Park at 6th Line in Nassagaweya and Pineridge Dr. Enter the forest on the trail that is directly opposite Pineridge Dr.

2. When I walked this section with a friend, we heard a loon, which was very Canadian. For the next 4.5k the trail takes you through young and mature

*A "huddle" of mushrooms trying to stay dry?*

hardwood forests, and dank cedar woods. You skirt farmers' fields, pass by small wetlands and climb a ridge that looks out over a hummocky moraine. You even walk along the old rail line for a short time and cross several rickety bridges over small, clear streams. Hiking bliss.

3. When you come to Dublin Line (the 1st road you come to), turn around and return to 6th Line and your car following the same route.

# Halton Forest Multiple Options Loop
## (Milton)

## OVERVIEW

I set out on this loop with an illegible map of trails that traversed a series of 5 forest tracts that are managed by Halton Region, and which are known collectively as the Halton Regional Forest Complex. In total, it covers about 400ha of contiguous forest, all of which is about 80 years old and consists of maple, basswood, birch, cherry and oak, with a few pines and spruce trees added for winter colour.

There is no climb to a vista or scramble to a waterfall; instead, you have up to 5 hours of uninterrupted walking in a spectacular forest. I startled a deer and saw 5 garter snakes, a big leopard frog and hundreds of chipmunks and squirrels. The birds were chirping, and a light breeze in the shady forest kept me cool. A couple who tested this route said, "That is one great hike! We loved it — quiet, green, easy." It's a great choice if you aren't sure how far you want to walk, because there are 3 options ranging from 5k to almost 15k. Each one is presented in the directions below.

Note that there are lots of smaller trails that you should ignore while keeping an eye open for mountain bikes.

## Nicola's
# Insider Info

**LENGTH**
14.4 kilometres
(9k and 5k options)

**LEVEL OF DIFFICULTY**
Easy

**LENGTH OF TIME**
3.5 to 5 hours
(2.25 to 3 hours)
(1.25 to 1.75 hours)

**NUMBER OF STEPS**
18,188

**kCAL BURNED** 560

**HIGHLIGHTS**
More than 14k of uninterrupted and peaceful forest walking, optional distances

**PLACES TO EAT/DRINK**
In Milton: Cup of Love (inside the Milton Mall) says "It's coffee o'clock," while the Make Café offers hot and cold lattes, along with smoothies and breakfast sandwiches. In Campbellville: The Flying Monkey Bike Shop & Coffee Bar has great espresso and desserts, while The Trail Eatery offers good downhome cooking.

**ENTRANCE FEE** n/a

**TRAILHEAD**
N43° 32.200′ W79° 58.711′

**BRUCE TRAIL MAP** 11

GPS
TRAIL MARKER
Loop 18

Halton Forest Multiple Options Loop

COX TRACT
BRITTON TRACT
Park at #10050.
Go straight onto Bruce Tr. side trail.
6th Line Nassagaweya
Leave Bruce Tr. side trail.

**Legend:**
- Trailhead
- Loop Route
- Interest Marker
- Direction Marker
- Main Bruce Trail
- Bruce Tr. Side Tr.
- Conservation Land:

GARTER SNAKES, CHIPMUNKS, RED SQUIRRELS & A DEER

Option 3 (5k) turnaround

ROBERTSON TRACT
4th Line
WHITE ROCK

Option 2 (9k) turnaround

MOUNTAIN BIKE DAREDEVIL TREE TRUNK

TURNER TRACT

HILTON FALLS CONSERVATION AREA

I LOVE WALKING ALONG BOARDWALKS.

THIS HEALTHY AIRY FOREST GOES ON AND ON.

Hilton Falls Reservoir

MAHON TRACT
Sideroad 10

CURRIE TRACT

Niagara Escarpment
Hwy 401

CERTIFIED FOREST

Sixteen Mile Creek
Campbellville Rd.

Guelph Line

Option 1 (14.4k) turnaround
Power Line

N
W E
S

0    0.5    1
Kilometres

*"Hiking makes me feel close to my Dad,*
*who is also hiking — in heaven."*

SANDRA GREEN

# Directions

1. Two parking lots provide access to the Britton Tract (1 of the 5 tracts you visit on the longest route) from 6th Line, just west and north of Milton. Park in the more southerly of the 2. Look for the green house number sign "10050."

2. Walk past the barrier on what is a road-like trail. This width and quality of trail keeps up until you come to 4th Line and could likely be navigated by a wheelchair or stroller. Harder going than on a paved trail, but it's reasonably flat and wide.

*This loop takes you through kilometres of this glorious airy forest.*

3. Almost immediately you see the blue blazes of the Bruce Tr.'s Hilton Falls Side Tr. DO NOT turn left, stay on the wider trail going straight. Blue blazes appear in this direction as well.

4. Cross over a creek, and when you come to a trail intersection after about 500m, leave the Bruce Tr. side trail by veering left onto a well-used path.

5. The trail runs deep inside an airy forest with a high canopy that allows light to filter through. If I were to put a human age on the trees, I'd say they were in their mid-30s. They are healthy, robust and brimming with life and dreams of the future. There were trilliums and jack-in-the-pulpits, and between splashes of wild ginger, fruit sprouted from mayapples and blue cohosh.

6. About 1k after you left the blue blazes, there is an intersection of trails that are signposted. This is your 1st decision point. (Skip past the Longest Option for Shorter Option directions.)

## Longest Option (14.4k) & Long Option (9k total hike)

7. Veer left and enter the Robertson Tract.

8. Though this trail is only occasionally signposted, for the most part it's not difficult to follow. It meanders through the forest where the birds chirped while squirrels and chipmunks (both members of the rodent family) rustled the leaves as they chased each other. Red squirrels (smaller with less bushy tails) and grey squirrels (which can also be black) eat birds' eggs and little chicks.

9. After another 2k, the trail exits onto 4th Line. This is your 2nd decision point. (Skip past the Longest Option for continuation of Longer, 9k Option directions.)

## Longest Option (14.4k total hike)

10. Turn left onto 4th Line.

11. Walk along 4th Line for about 400m until the road turns sharply to the right and becomes 10th Sideroad. Look for a trail that re-enters the forest to your left (at street address #3990), just past the last of several reflective road signs. You are entering the Mahon Tract.

12. When you come to a T-intersection of trails, go right and then at a Y-intersection of trails, veer left down onto the first of several boardwalks.

13. Along this section of trail, I spied a beautiful leopard frog. Seeing one of these amphibians is good since they are a "canary in the coal mine." Frogs do poorly in polluted water, so their presence indicates the water is clean.

14. Cross under the power line and re-enter the forest. The forest thins a bit, with pines and spruce replacing the more leafy hardwoods. It has a much more open feel to it.

15. When you come to a parking lot on Guelph Line (street address #9475), which is another 3k past your last decision point at 4th Line, you really do have to turn around and begin your return trip. But don't fear — there is new territory ahead.

*Frogs indicate the water is clean.*
PHOTO BY GILL STEAD

*Trilliums.* PHOTO BY BETT LEVERETTE

16. You are now in the Currie Tract, which is a Certified Forest within the Eastern Ontario Model Forest group (EOMF). According to its website, "The EOMF champions the belief that we all have a stake in ensuring that the environmental, economic, cultural and social values of eastern Ontario's forests are maintained for the benefit of all, now and in the future."

17. Retrace the trail you came in on until you come to a T-intersection of trails, where you turn right. If you arrive back at the 4th Line/10th Sideroad you have missed this turn so retrace your footsteps. You are now in the Turner Tract. Cross a small stream. Ignore the bike paths and stay on the main trail.

18. At the next Y-intersection of trails, veer left.

19. At the 2nd of a couple of spots where the mountain bikers play daredevil riding along a fallen tree trunk, keep going straight, with the fallen tree trunk on your right.

20. At the next Y-intersection of trails, veer right.

21. The next intersection is a T-intersection, where you turn right and rejoin a wider trail that you came in on. I stopped here for a drink of water on a nice, flat-topped rock. A couple of cyclists came by and explained that this was the "white rock," which is a landmark along this stretch of trail.

22. You return to an intersection of trails you've visited before. There is a trail sign here. Turn left.

23. I startled a deer just past here as the trail opened onto a big wetland.

24. At the next signposted intersection of trails, go right, picking up the blue blazes of the Hilton Falls Side Tr. (the blazes go in both directions).

25. A short 1k later, you come to your last intersection of trails. Turn left here and return to your car.

## Long Option
### (9k total hike)

1. Continued from Point #9 above.

2. Turn around and retrace your footsteps for 2k until you arrive back at an intersection of trails you've visited before. There is a trail sign here. Turn left.

*The very dark, scaly bark is characteristic of this black cherry.*

3. I startled a deer just past here as the trail opened onto a big wetland.

4. At the next signposted intersection of trails, go right, picking up the blue blazes of the Hilton Falls Side Tr. (the blazes go in both directions).

5. A short 1k later, you come to your last intersection of trails. Turn left here and return to your car.

## Shorter Option
### (5k total hike)

1. Continued from Point #6 above.

2. Veer right.

3. At the next signposted intersection of trails, go right, picking up the blue blazes of the Hilton Falls Side Tr. (the blazes go in both directions).

4. A short 1k later, you come to your last intersection of trails. Turn left here and return to your car.

# Hendrie Valley Loop
## (Burlington)

## OVERVIEW

The Royal Botanical Gardens (RBG) is a gem of gigantic proportions. Covering 1,100ha that straddle the border between Burlington and Hamilton, the RBG has 27k of hiking trails. And if this 7.2k loop is any indication, you should definitely plan to visit. Much of this route goes along raised boardwalks through expansive marshes. Birds, insects, fish and small mammals abound.

This loop passes by Laking Garden, and then follows a quiet trail alongside the enormous Grindstone Marshes. There are great interpretive signs, one of which explains that the buildup of sediment is a big threat to this floodplain ecosystem. In earlier times, it received a hit of sediment once a year during spring runoff. Now, industrial and residential development, agriculture and the trend toward more violent storms also add sediment. The trail continues alongside Grindstone Creek, and after about 4.5k arrives at a great picnic spot. If you do the shorter 3.9k route, you miss the picnic area but still get to enjoy the boardwalks and marshes. I was stunned by how away-from-it-all this trail seems to be. The person who tested this hike saw a muskrat — its telltale, rat-like tail propelling it along in the water.

### Nicola's
# Insider Info

**LENGTH**
7.2 kilometres
(3.9k option)

**LEVEL OF DIFFICULTY**
Easy

**LENGTH OF TIME**
1.75 to 2.5 hours
(1 to 1.5 hours)

**NUMBER OF STEPS** 9,723

**kCAL BURNED** 296

**HIGHLIGHTS**
Boardwalks through marshes, friendly squirrels & chipmunks galore, waterfowl, water plants, water, water, water

**PLACES TO EAT/DRINK**
Hiker Mike gives a thumbs up to the Lola Choco Bar and Sweet House. For all you Bosnians, they also serve Bosnian coffee. The mum and daughter duo at Kelly's Bake Shoppe bake up some amazing treats, including vegan and gluten-free cupcakes and cookies.

**PARKING FEE** $3.00/hour or day pass $16.00

**TRAILHEAD**
N43° 17.534' W79° 53.177'

GPS

TRAIL MARKER
Loop 19

Free Parking
Antony P Wheaton
1939-2002
Love Always

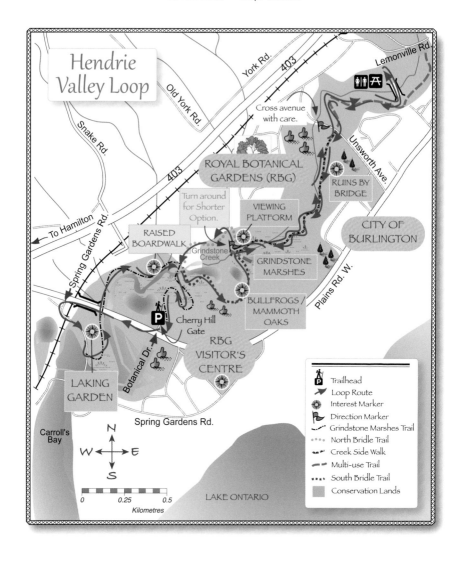

## Hendrie Valley Loop

York Rd.

403

Lemonville Rd.

Old York Rd.

Snake Rd.

403

To Hamilton

Spring Gardens Rd.

Cross avenue with care.

ROYAL BOTANICAL GARDENS (RBG)

Turn around for Shorter Option.

VIEWING PLATFORM

RAISED BOARDWALK

Grindstone Creek

GRINDSTONE MARSHES

BULLFROGS / MAMMOTH OAKS

Cherry Hill Gate

RBG VISITOR'S CENTRE

Botanical Dr.

LAKING GARDEN

Carroll's Bay

Spring Gardens Rd.

Unsworth Ave.

RUINS BY BRIDGE

CITY OF BURLINGTON

Plains Rd. W.

N
W ←→ E
S

0    0.25    0.5
Kilometres

LAKE ONTARIO

### Legend

- **P** Trailhead
- Loop Route
- Interest Marker
- Direction Marker
- Grindstone Marshes Trail
- North Bridle Trail
- Creek Side Walk
- Multi-use Trail
- South Bridle Trail
- Conservation Lands

"It's wonderful to spend time with the locals as you hike through their country. They are so proud of what they have and wish to tell you so much about their homeland: the history, the terrain, the weather. When you are hiking, you get to stop and smell the roses (not to mention the cuisine)."

BARBARA KARASIUK

# Directions

1.  Park in the Cherry Hill Gate/Hendrie Valley parking lot. It's on Plains Rd. at Botanical Dr., opposite the Esquire Motel, and not far from the RBG Visitor Centre. You can pay to park by the hour or, if you intend to visit the gardens, go to the Visitor Centre and buy a day pass that includes parking.

2.  Leave the parking lot and cross Plains Rd. at the traffic light. Turn right onto Plains Rd. and cross the high bridge over railway tracks. This is the only stretch of road on the loop, and you get it over with right away.

3.  After you cross the bridge, turn left onto Spring Gardens Rd., cross the parking lot and cross back over the railway tracks on the pedestrian bridge.

4.  When you come to the small road on the other side of the tracks, turn right and head downhill. You pass by Laking Garden.

5.  At the bottom of the hill, look for a large signboard on your left. The Grindstone Marshes Tr. begins here. Go past the sign, following the trail, with the marshes to your right.

6.  After 800m, you come to a raised boardwalk that extends for the next 350m.

7.  Pass by the junction for Bridle Tr. (North) by veering to the right and going over a metal bridge — I got up close and personal with a black squirrel here.

8.  When the boardwalk ends, turn left onto Bridle Tr. (South). I could hear bullfrogs and spied a big fat garter snake. I also spied some oak trees with huge girths along this stretch of trail.

*People feed these very friendly squirrels.*

9.  At the next trail intersection, turn left following the sign that says "to Creek Side Walk" and look for the viewing platform.

10. Shortly afterwards, you come to another trail intersection, where Creek Side Walk goes to your right. At this point you have a decision to make about whether you want to complete the longer 7.2k route or the shorter, 3.9k option.

*There are kilometres of fabulous boardwalks through the Grindstone Marshes.*

## Longer Option **(7.2k total hike)**

11. Turn right onto Creek Side Walk and cross the creek as the trail narrows. This section of trail is on red Queenston shale that is reportedly very slippery in the spring. The red clay is a good indicator that you are on the Niagara Escarpment. For those of you who know the Cheltenham Badlands near Caledon, this is the same formation.

12. You cross the creek again, and there are structures along the riverbank that remind us that this area was once an industrial one.

13. Cross Unsworth Ave. (where there is free parking) and enter Hidden Valley Park. For the next 600m you follow the Multi-Use Tr., which is wider and paved. It continues alongside the creek until you come to a bridge on your left that crosses into a small park where there are picnic tables, a playground and washrooms.

14. When you are ready, retrace your footsteps on the Multi-Use Tr. to Unsworth Ave., and then on Creek Side Walk to the intersection with Bridle Tr. (North). Turn right onto Bridle Tr. (North), cross over a small bridge in a nice shady spot where there is a bench that I couldn't resist. There are some American plane, or sycamore, trees here. You can recognize them by their smooth,

spotty bark. They have maple-like leaves, and their fruit is ball-shaped and about 1.5cm in diameter. They grow throughout Ontario, but I've not seen a lot of them.

15. Walk along the boardwalk and then leave the water, walking up and then down into the forest. At the trail intersection on the next boardwalk, turn left onto the Grindstone Marshes Tr. and cross the bridge that you crossed earlier in the day.

16. At the end of this boardwalk, go right and uphill this time. Then veer right toward Cherry Hill and your car.

*An American plane or American sycamore tree.*

## Shorter Option (3.9k total hike)

1. Continued from Point #10 above.

2. Keep going straight at the intersection where Creek Side Walk goes to the right. You follow Bridle Tr. (North).

3. Cross over a small bridge in a nice shady spot where there is a bench that I couldn't resist. There are some American plane, or sycamore, trees here. You can recognize them by their smooth spotty bark. They have maple-like leaves, and their fruit is ball-shaped and about 1.5cm in diameter. They grow throughout Ontario, but I've not seen a lot of them.

*Garter snakes have a vomeronasal system that allows them to smell via their tongue.*

PHOTO BY SAHA CHATTERPAUL

4. Walk along the boardwalk and then leave the water, walking up and then down into the forest. At the trail intersection on the next boardwalk, turn left onto the Grindstone Marshes Tr. and cross the bridge that you crossed earlier in the day.

5. At the end of this boardwalk, go right and uphill this time. Then veer right toward Cherry Hill and your car.

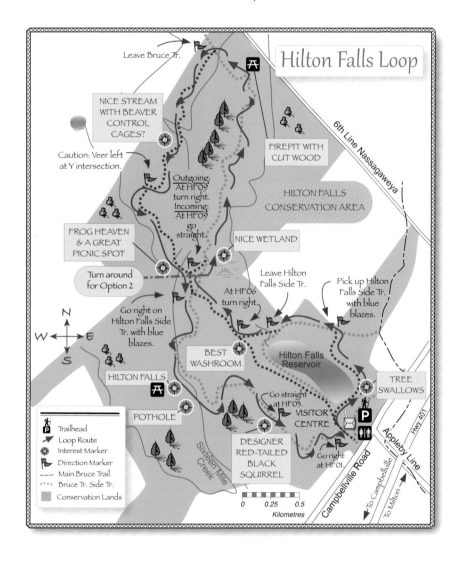

# Hilton Falls Loop

Leave Bruce Tr.

6th Line Nassagaweya

NICE STREAM WITH BEAVER CONTROL CAGES?

Caution: Veer left at Y intersection.

FIREPIT WITH CUT WOOD

HILTON FALLS CONSERVATION AREA

Outgoing: At HF09 turn right. Incoming: At HF09 go straight.

FROG HEAVEN & A GREAT PICNIC SPOT

NICE WETLAND

Turn around for Option 2

Leave Hilton Falls Side Tr.

Pick up Hilton Falls Side Tr. with blue blazes.

At HF06 turn right.

Go right on Hilton Falls Side Tr. with blue blazes.

BEST WASHROOM

Hilton Falls Reservoir

TREE SWALLOWS

HILTON FALLS

POTHOLE

Go straight at HF03.

VISITOR CENTRE

Go right at HF01.

DESIGNER RED-TAILED BLACK SQUIRREL

Sixteen Mile Creek

N
W — E
S

Appleby Line
Hwy 401
To Campbellville
To Milton
Campbellville Road

**Legend:**
- Trailhead
- Loop Route
- Interest Marker
- Direction Marker
- Main Bruce Trail
- Bruce Tr. Side Tr.
- Conservation Lands

0   0.25   0.5
Kilometres

*"Life is about relationships, and one of the most important relationships is the one with the Earth, which is our home. Hiking nourishes that relationship for me."*

CATHERINE PLEY

# Hilton Falls Loop (Campbellville)

*This route is a bit tricky so be alert! If you miss
a turn, just backtrack. The letter signs help.
Currently, you require a reservation to visit the
Hilton Falls Conservation Area. You can book
two-hour slots at www.conservationhalton.ca.*

## OVERVIEW

He Hilton Falls Conservation Area covers
a large area and has great trails with
lots to see. If you hike the longer, 10.8k
version, you will need to arrange back-to-back,
2-hour passes. For the 6.5k route, one time slot
should do it.

Part of Sixteen Mile Creek, the waterfall was
created by receding glaciers some 12,000 years
ago. Early settlers in the 1830s realized this site's
potential for producing the hydropower needed
for grist- and sawmills. Ruins of an old mill remain.
When one visits sites like this, it's easy to just see
the pretty waterfall and skim the information
presented on interpretive signs. But take a moment
to imagine this now quiet cedar forest on the edge
of cliff as a vibrant town with mills and stores and
homes. There would have been streets, or at least
rutted roads, with horses pulling carts loaded with
wheat to be milled or massive tree trunks to be
sawn. Rather than birds, you'd hear neighbours
welcoming each other. The site would have been
stripped of its trees and open to the cliffs. It's hard,
but just possible, to imagine.

> **Conservation Halton**
> **(www.conservationhalton.ca)** *encourages you and
> your family to enjoy the trails at all of our parks.*

## Nicola's
# Insider Info

**LENGTH**
10.8 kilometres
(6.5k option)

**LEVEL OF DIFFICULTY**
Moderate

**LENGTH OF TIME**
2.5 to 3.5 hours
(1.5 to 2 hours)

**NUMBER OF STEPS**
14,909

**kCAL BURNED** 460

**HIGHLIGHTS**
Hilton Falls, pothole,
outhouse, reservoir,
stuffed beaver, fire pits
with chopped wood

**PLACES TO EAT/DRINK**
Park Visitor Centre/
Flying Monkey Bike Shop
& Coffee Bar, The Trail
Eatery in Campbellville/
Lowville Bistro in Lowville

**ENTRANCE FEE**
Adult $9.50/Senior (65+)
$7.50/Child (5–14) $6.50/
Child (<5) free

**HOURS** Park opens at
8:30am daily

**TRAILHEAD**
N43° 30.341'W79° 57.704'

**BRUCE TRAIL MAP** 11

TRAIL MARKER
Loop 20

# Directions

1. From the parking lot, make your way to the Visitor Centre. There are washrooms inside and a small collection of stuffed wild animals, including a stuffed beaver. Give him or her (believe me, you don't want to know how biologists tell the difference between beaver genders, though I will tell you it involves one's nose) a big pat. I love beavers, and give a talk about them called "Love Thy Beaver."

2. From the Visitor Centre, walk uphill toward the forest. When you come to a small road, turn right and follow it toward the Hilton Falls Reservoir.

3. Go past the reservoir and continue along the small road as it climbs up gently. When we walked here, tree swallows were swooping by at eye level so you could see their iridescent blue backs. Gorgeous.

4. After about 1k, you come to the Hilton Falls Side Tr., which is part of the Bruce Tr. Go straight, following the blue blazes of the Hilton Falls Side Tr.

5. Continue following the road until you come to a trail intersection marked "HF06." Along the way, you will have left the Hilton Falls Side Tr. and passed by an example of how to really use a culvert!

6. At sign "HF06," go right. The purple arrows on the signpost show you are following the Beaver Dam Tr. You will be following this trail for the next 6k.

7. The trail crosses the Hilton Falls Side Tr. again before coming to sign "HF09." This is where you have to decide between the longer 10.8k option and the shorter 6.5k route.

## Longer Option (10.8k total hike)

8. Turn right at sign "HF09." Shortly, the Hilton Falls Side Tr. joins the Beaver Dam Tr. Follow the blue blazes of the Hilton Falls Side Tr.

9. Pass by some lovely wetlands where we had to be careful not to step on the frogs that kept leaping in our way. The forest becomes more mature and beautiful, and the wider road gives way to a narrower path.

*There were frogs galore.*

*Trees of life.*

I noticed how the narrow paths, which are typical of the Bruce Tr., give you a more intimate hiking experience than the wider ones often used by conservation areas. See what you think. Along here, there is also a fabulous picnic area with a table and fire pit with firewood supplied.

10. When you come to the spot where the Hilton Falls Side Tr. peels off to the right from the Beaver Dam Tr., stay left on the latter trail. You are beginning your return trip.

11. Stick with the Beaver Dam Tr. all the way around a big 5k loop, passing HF13 and HF20, which show the Beaver Dam Tr.'s purple arrows. Pass by the Wally and the Beav cycling trail, then come to a boardwalk and bridge near another great picnic spot — and more frogs.

12. At sign "HF09," turn right as indicated by the signpost arrow.

13. A very short 200m later, go right onto the Hilton Falls Side Tr. with its blue blazes. It would be easy to miss this turn, so eyes open again, because if you miss it, you miss the waterfall and pothole, too. You leave the Beaver Dam Tr. at this point.

14. You come to the lovely Sixteen Mile Creek and follow it to the waterfall. This is a great place to stop for lunch. There are picnic tables, a fire pit and firewood and the falls. This is the highlight of this loop, so take some time to enjoy it. You deserve the break. As I suggested in the Overview, try to imagine this spot with a mill, houses and horses. Our pioneers were hearty souls; there's no doubt.

15. When you continue on, keep following the blue blazes of the Bruce Tr. side trail over some rocky terrain through a fine cedar forest. I lived for a time in Calgary and found I missed these cedar forests. Also called swamp cedars because they love having wet feet, Eastern white cedars (*Thuja occidentalis*)

are also called arborvitae, which means "tree of life." This latter name was apparently coined by Jacques Cartier in the 1500s after he learned from the Iroquois that it could be used to cure scurvy.

16. Shortly, you pass by a "pothole." A sign explains how this impossibly round hole was created by natural forces. Amazing.

17. Cross the 1st road you come to, and then turn right on the 2nd road, following the Hilton Falls Side Tr.'s blue blazes.

18. At sign "HF03," go straight, leaving the Hilton Falls Side Tr.'s blue blazes. We spied a very stylish and unusual black squirrel with a red tail here.

*Hilton Falls.*

19. At sign "HF01," go right, and then veer right at the Y-intersection of trails, heading downhill.

20. Cross the road and return to the Visitor Centre.

## Shorter Option **(6.5k total hike)**

1. Continued from Point #9 above.

2. At sign "HF09," turn around and head back along the same trail.

3. Go to Point #15 above.

# "Hole in the Wall"
# Figure Eight Loop (Limehouse)

## OVERVIEW

If you want to combine fascinating history with a potpourri of natural landscapes, this loop is for you. Similarly, if you are walking with cliff-savvy kids, this is a wonderful choice. I'd be giving it away if I told you too much about the lime kilns, the archway, the "hole in the wall," the enormous maples and white pines and the fields of goldenrod (in fall) that you'll encounter en route. But expect kids and adults alike to be wowed while walking this figure-8 loop. The shorter, 3.6k option, which completes only the second half of the figure 8, may be the better choice with kids.

Limehouse was a hub of industrial activity in the later part of the 19th century after lime was discovered nearby. The quiet village once had a woolen mill, a sawmill and a paint works, and it was a main stop along the Grand Trunk Railway. Studies indicate the Limehouse Conservation Area is home to a number of species at risk, including bobolinks, golden-winged warblers, Canada warblers and Eastern meadowlarks. You can find endangered butternut trees and it supports 14 dragonfly and damselfly species, 2 of which are endangered: the swamp spreadwing and the sweetflag spreadwing.

*If you want to enjoy hiking in Halton from your doorstep, contact **Jill Johnson** at Royal LePage Meadowtowne Realty (905-873-5592). Read about her hiking for charity activities at **www.jilljohnson.ca**.*

**21**

### Nicola's
## Insider Info

**LENGTH**
7.2 kilometres
(3.6k option)

**LEVEL OF DIFFICULTY**
Moderate

**LENGTH OF TIME**
1.75 to 2.5 hours
(1 to 1.5 hours)

**NUMBER OF STEPS**
9,564

**kCAL BURNED** 339

**HIGHLIGHTS**
Open landscape, monarch butterflies, lime kilns, archway, "hole in the wall," village of Limehouse

**PLACES TO EAT/DRINK**
Heather's Bakery, Silvercreek Socialhaus, The St. George Pub, Symposium Café Restaurant & Lounge in Georgetown

**ENTRANCE FEE** n/a

**TRAILHEAD**
N43° 38.297' W79° 58.742'

**BRUCE TRAIL MAP** 12

GPS

### TRAIL MARKER
Loop 21

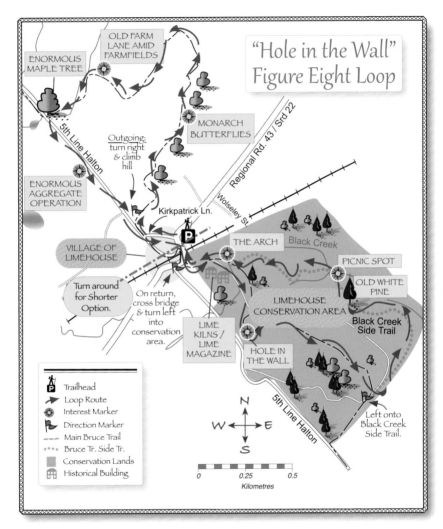

"Hole in the Wall" Figure Eight Loop

ENORMOUS MAPLE TREE

OLD FARM LANE AMID FARMFIELDS

MONARCH BUTTERFLIES

5th Line Halton

Outgoing; turn right & climb hill

Regional Rd. 43 / Srd 22

ENORMOUS AGGREGATE OPERATION

Kirkpatrick Ln.

Wolseley St.

VILLAGE OF LIMEHOUSE

THE ARCH    Black Creek

PICNIC SPOT

OLD WHITE PINE

Turn around for Shorter Option.

On return, cross bridge & turn left into conservation area.

LIMEHOUSE CONSERVATION AREA

Black Creek Side Trail

LIME KILNS / LIME MAGAZINE

HOLE IN THE WALL

5th Line Halton

Left onto Black Creek Side Trail.

**Legend**

- 🏕 Trailhead
- ➤ Loop Route
- ✺ Interest Marker
- ⚑ Direction Marker
- --- Main Bruce Trail
- •••• Bruce Tr. Side Tr.
- ▪ Conservation Lands
- ⌂ Historical Building

N
W — E
S

0    0.25    0.5
Kilometres

## Directions

*Note that this route requires some scrambling over a rocky area near the "hole in the wall."*

### Longer Option (7.2k total hike)

1. There is public parking on the east side of the village of Limehouse. From there, walk west into Limehouse.

2. Look for little Kirkpatrick Lane, on the east side of the bridge and take it. Follow the white blazes of the main Bruce Tr.

*Eastern tiger swallowtail butterflies.* PHOTO BY NICK MARSHALL

3. Kirkpatrick Lane passes by some lovely heritage homes before ending at 5th Line. Cross 5th Line, turn left and follow 5th Line for a very brief 60m, keeping your eyes open for where the trail leaves the road on your right.

4. Climb up briefly, stay left at a fork in the trail and then for the next 2k, follow a well-worn trail with white blazes that eventually skirts farm fields. At times, the path passes through what were once farm lanes that separated fields before these corridors were removed to accommodate increasingly large farm machinery. This is a pity since, like the hedgerows in the UK, these lanes provided habitat for birds and animals, created transportation corridors and buffered crops from wind.

5. There is a lot of milkweed — the favoured food of monarch caterpillars — nearby. For those interested, butterflies and moths have a lot in common, but the easiest way to tell them apart is by their antennae. Butterflies have club-shaped antennae with bulbous ends, whereas moths have feathery ones. Generally, though it's not always the case, butterflies tend to be active during the day; moths like the night.

6. Bypass the Todd Vardes Meadowland Side Tr.

7. Where the trail drops down and crosses a stream, I came across a gathering of robins. It being November, it seemed late for these migratory birds. But it turns out that many robins overwinter in Ontario. When they do, they travel in flocks when in search of food.

*"Hole in the wall."*

8. Just before the trail comes back out onto 5th Line, there is an enormous maple tree. I'd give it 200 years or more.

9. Turn left onto 5th Line, leaving the Bruce Tr. Walk along this quiet road for less than 1k. Look right to see the mammoth aggregate operations that surround Limehouse.

10. When you arrive back in Limehouse, pick up the Bruce Tr's white blazes, following them down Kirkpatrick Lane.

11. At the far end of Kirkpatrick Lane, turn right, cross the bridge and make a sharp left turn into the Limehouse Conservation Area.

12. Make sure you read the great interpretive signs before proceeding into Limehouse's industrial past.

13. Take time to explore the small trails that leave the main path and lead you to ruins of a powder magazine, where explosives were stored, and a large lime kiln. There is also a smaller, preserved lime kiln. They are concrete evidence of what went on years ago.

14. Cross a little bridge over Black Creek. Look upstream and there is an archway with a keystone that has held this primitive bridge in place for 100 years or more.

15. Pass by the turn-off for the Black Creek Side Tr., sticking with the main Bruce Tr.'s white blazes.

*Arch over Black Creek.*

16. Turn right after the bridge, continuing to follow the Bruce Tr.'s white blazes. A little further along, climb up into a rocky, forested area that is damp and slippery with moss. This is the "hole in the wall" and it's a great spot. You'll see.

17. The trail continues along a ridge on a path lined with large, flat stones. Pass by a trail that leads to a parking area on your right.

18. When you come to a 2nd junction with the Black Creek Side Tr., take it. Follow its blue blazes to the left, leaving the main Bruce Tr.'s white blazes. Don't miss a sharp right-hand turn.

19. The path drops into the valley and follows Black Creek. There is a great picnic spot near the stream.

20. When you arrive at the intersection with the main Bruce Tr., turn right and follow its white blazes.

21. Pass over the bridge by the arch and the lime kilns on your return to the village of Limehouse and your car.

## Shorter Option (3.6k total hike)

1. There is public parking on the east side of the village of Limehouse. From there, walk west into Limehouse.

2. Enter the Limehouse Conservation Area by the entrance, right by the railway tracks in Limehouse.

3. Go to Point #12 above.

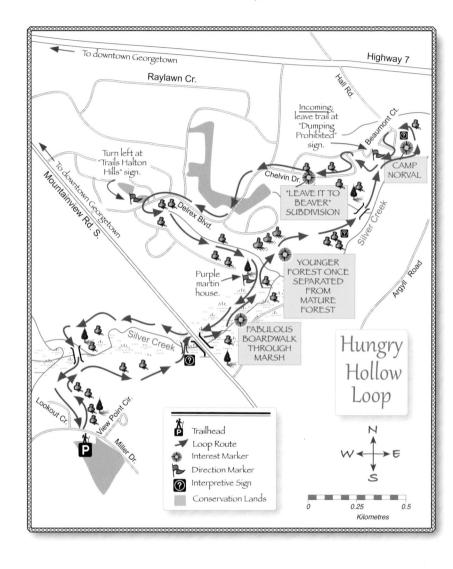

**Hungry Hollow Loop**

Legend:
- Trailhead
- Loop Route
- Interest Marker
- Direction Marker
- Interpretive Sign
- Conservation Lands

Raylawn Cr.

To downtown Georgetown

Highway 7

Hall Rd.

Incoming: leave trail at "Dumping Prohibited" sign.

Beaumont Ct.

CAMP NORVAL

Chelvin Dr.

Turn left at "Trails Halton Hills" sign.

To downtown Georgetown

Mountainview Rd. S.

Delrex Blvd.

"LEAVE IT TO BEAVER" SUBDIVISION

Silver Creek

YOUNGER FOREST ONCE SEPARATED FROM MATURE FOREST

Argyll Road

Purple martin house.

Silver Creek

FABULOUS BOARDWALK THROUGH MARSH

Lookout Cr.

View Point Cir.

Miller Dr.

N
W — E
S

0     0.25     0.5
Kilometres

*"As a senior, I realize that through hiking I can continue to challenge myself and still have the same kind of fun the younger me enjoyed!"*

TORY McMAHON

# Hungry Hollow Loop
## (Georgetown)

## OVERVIEW

Atter spending the winter in Mexico — where I did some great hiking, I might add — I returned to home-sweet-snowy-home at the end of March. An April snowstorm gave me the opportunity to get out on the trails and enjoy the white stuff. My companion and I walked this one on a crisp day. The sky was blue, there was no wind and by mid-afternoon we had shed our toques. The snow stayed a pristine white in the sub-zero temperature. This route follows Silver Creek, and it was roaring as though it was a river and not merely a creek. The earth smelled like life, and the spring robins mixed with chickadees and cardinals in an April chorus. Glorious. It was as if Canada wanted me to embrace winter, even though it was technically spring.

If you live in or near Georgetown, this hike is a must. If you live some way from Georgetown, it's worth a drive. Hungry Hollow is a hidden gem. It's a deep valley that courses through one of southern Ontario's prettier towns, but for the most part Georgetown is out-of-sight and out-of-mind. You're in an oasis of forest and marsh and water.

*If you want to enjoy hiking in Halton from your doorstep, contact Jill Johnson at Royal LePage Meadowtowne Realty (905-873-5592). Read about her hiking for charity activities at www.jilljohnson.ca.*

### Nicola's Insider Info

**LENGTH**
7.8 kilometres

**LEVEL OF DIFFICULTY**
Easy

**LENGTH OF TIME**
2 to 2.5 hours

**NUMBER OF STEPS**
9,367

**kCAL BURNED** 307

**HIGHLIGHTS**
Wilderness in a city, Silver Creek, boardwalks

**PLACES TO EAT/DRINK**
Heather's Bakery, Silvercreek Socialhaus, The St. George Pub, Symposium Café Restaurant & Lounge in Georgetown

**ENTRANCE FEE**
n/a

**TRAILHEAD**
N43° 38.024'W79° 53.617'

**TRAIL MARKER**
Loop 22

*It sure doesn't look like spring-flower season.*

# Directions

1. Park on Miller Dr., between Lookout Ct. and View Point Cir., beside a fenced-off wooded area. Find the opening that allows you to enter the forest. There are several signs, one of which says "Trails Halton Hills."

2. Follow the trail to the 1st fork, where you veer left (straight). When you come to a bench, veer left again, as the trail drops into the valley.

3. When you arrive in the valley bottom, bear right and right again, so you follow the trail, keeping Silver Creek on your left (though it's not really visible yet).

4. The trail follows the pretty valley bottom, coming to the high overpass for Mountainview Rd. In the shadow of the overpass, there is a sign about fish species. Turn left, cross the bridge over Silver Creek, and on the other side of the stream turn right, passing under the overpass.

5. Silver Creek flows into the Credit River. As you'll have read on the sign, it's home to brook and rainbow trout and also an endangered species called redside dace. The endangered label means it's facing imminent risk of extinction or extirpation. Since loss of suitable habitat as a result of agriculture and urbanization is causing problems for this member of the minnow family, the fact that they have been found in the middle of Georgetown indicates that Silver Creek is in good health.

6. For the next 500m, follow a boardwalk through a lovely marshy area with the creek in clear view (at least it was clearly visible before the leaves were out). The bulrushes had been ravaged by snow and ice, but the chickadees weren't put off by their ragged appearance. The cardinals were less shy than normal, likely because the showy red males were particularly interested in being seen by potential mates. Spring was bursting.

7. As the boardwalk ends, the trail veers left away from the creek. When you come to an intersection of trails where there is a large purple martin

birdhouse, veer right and then right again. The trail heads up the far side of   the valley, back into some trees.

8. While on the topic of purple martins, I read that these birds don't eat 2,000 mosquitoes a day as birdhouse manufacturers suggest. This sales pitch came from a researcher who discovered about 2,000 mosquitoes in the stomachs of purple martins. But these were the larger, saltwater marsh mosquitoes found in Louisiana, not the little ones we despise in Ontario. Local research indicates purple martins eat most kinds of flying insects, and that mosquitoes may make up only about 2% of their diet.

9. At the top of the valley, stay right and enter a forest made up of apple and thorn trees with the odd young maple. This area likely was once pasture for cattle that would have spread the seeds. The small-diameter trees soon give way to a mature forest. At one time, there must have been a fence that kept livestock out of the older trees, allowing the trees to flourish. See if you can find it.

10. Veer left at the fork in the trail just before an interpretive sign about vegetation. You're now walking along a ridge with valleys on both sides.

11. Cross over a long bridge that spans a deep ravine with a small stream in it.

12. Houses begin to appear on your left as you walk along a lovely trail that comes to a sign announcing that this area used to be Camp Norval. You can read about the camp's history and try to imagine all the old cabins, the swimming pool and dining hall.

13. The trail loops around and you come to a fork. Stay left and follow the trail along a ridge above Silver Creek. Leaving the trees behind, enter a brand-spanking-new subdivision. This rather exclusive subdivision has enormous houses that virtually fill the lot, leaving minimal

*The beautiful stones look like they came from the Niagara Escarpment and have been there for some time.*

space for grass or trees. Keep the image of this subdivision in mind because I'll ask you to call upon it later.

14. Walk across Hall Rd., going straight ahead on Beaumont Ct. Right after #33 Beaumont Ct., look for an opening in the fence on your right with signage for the trail.

15. Pass through the opening, turn right onto the trail and re-enter the forest. This is actually the same trail that you took to get here.

16. Keep your eyes open for a trail — really more of a grassy area — on your right, that passes between 2 fenced-in backyards. Turn right and follow it, leaving the cinder trail. There is a sign on your left that says "Dumping Prohibited."

17. The trail goes up a gentle incline, swinging to the left before coming out onto a street. There is no street sign, but this is Chelvin Dr.

18. Turn left and follow Chelvin Dr. as it bends left.

19. Now recall the subdivision on Beaumont Ct. Note that in this older subdivision, the houses are smaller so there is room for a yard and big trees. The feel of these 2 subdivisions is very different. As you follow Chelvin Dr., you almost expect the characters of *Leave it to Beaver* to come walking down the street. There is a calmness that I think is due to the green space and trees.

20. When you come to Delrex Blvd., turn left. You have to follow this busier road for under 1k before you get back down into the forest calm.

21. When the forest joins the roadside on your left and is separated by a wire fence, look for a sign that says "Trails Halton Hills." Turn left here and re-enter the forest. The trail drops down into the valley.

22. When you come to the intersection of trails with the purple martin house, go straight ahead toward Silver Creek and retrace the route along the boardwalk.

23. Walk underneath the high overpass, and at the T-intersection of trails, turn right (do not go over the bridge). When the path forks, veer left. (The path to the right climbs up to Mountainview Rd.)

24. At the next intersection of trails, turn left toward Silver Creek and cross over the bridge.

25. After crossing the bridge, take the 2nd trail to the right, which is the trail that you came in on.

26. This trail climbs up to the mature forest before arriving at Miller Dr. and your car.

# Joshua's Creek South Loop
## (Oakville)

**Nicola's**
## Insider Info

**LENGTH**
6.5 kilometres

**LEVEL OF DIFFICULTY**
Easy

**LENGTH OF TIME**
1.5 to 2.5 hours

**NUMBER OF STEPS**
8,119

**kCAL BURNED** 252

**HIGHLIGHTS**
Naturalized Joshua's
Creek, lakeshore,
huge homes

**PLACES TO EAT/DRINK**
Tribeca Coffee Co. is a
great supporter of my
hiking guides and has
great coffee! Vereda
Central Coffee Roasters,
Monastery Bakery, Aroma
Espresso Bar, Bean There,
Kerr Street Café, Stoney's
Bread Co., Taste of
Colombia in Oakville

**ENTRANCE FEE** n/a

**TRAILHEAD**
N43° 28.771′ W79° 38.637′

## OVERVIEW

I walked this route with 28 members of the Pathfinders Hiking Group of Oakville. (**www.oakvillepathfinders.blogspot.ca**)

A member and avid hiker, Richard Olley told me the group usually has about 20 hikers on their regular Monday and Thursday hikes (September to June). The club has about 100 members — all of them seniors. Their hikes come in longer, medium and "turtles," so there is something for everyone. It was a spectacular spring day with cherry and apple blossoms, tulips, daffodils and blankets of stunning alyssum. The sun was out and so were the Pathfinders.

This hike follows Joshua's Creek through a forested area, skirts the lakeshore and passes by some enormous houses. As we returned, I asked Basanthy what the highlight of the hike had been for her. I expected this Oakville resident to tell me the walk along the lakeshore, but she had a different idea. Her favourite thing was the impressive rock garden behind one of the houses we passed by. The other was Joshua's Creek, which she described as peaceful. It made me realize that while the lakeshore is spectacular, this was Oakville, and the people who live here see the lake far more often than a gentle brook.

**TRAIL MARKER**
*Loop 23*

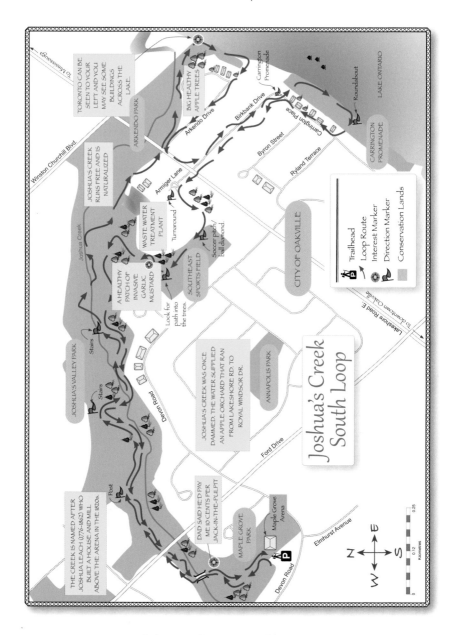

Joshua's Creek
South Loop

TORONTO CAN BE SEEN TO YOUR LEFT AND YOU MAY SEE SOME BUILDINGS ACROSS THE LAKE.

BIG HEALTHY APPLE TREES

JOSHUA'S CREEK RUNS FREE AND IS NATURALIZED

ARKENDO PARK

A HEALTHY PATCH OF INVASIVE GARLIC MUSTARD

WASTE WATER TREATMENT PLANT

Turnaround

SOUTHEAST SPORTS FIELD

Soccer pitch/ ball diamond.

Look for path into the trees.

JOSHUA'S VALLEY PARK

Stairs

Stairs

Post

THE CREEK IS NAMED AFTER JOSHUA LEACH (1776–1862) WHO BUILT A HOUSE AND MILL ABOVE THE ARENA IN THE 1820s.

DAD SAID HE'D PAY ME 10 CENTS PER JACK-IN-THE-PULPIT

JOSHUA'S CREEK WAS ONCE DAMMED. THE WATER SUPPLIED AN APPLE ORCHARD THAT RAN FROM LAKESHORE RD. TO ROYAL WINDSOR DR.

ANNAPOLIS PARK

MAPLE GROVE PARK

Maple Grove Arena

CITY OF OAKVILLE

To downtown Oakville

Lakeshore Road E.

Ford Drive

Elmhurst Avenue

Devon Road

Devon Road

Armiger Lane

Joshua Creek

Winston Churchill Blvd.

To Mississauga

Arkendo Drive

Birkbank Drive

Byron Street

Ryland Terrace

Carrington Place

Carrington Promenade

CARRINGTON PROMENADE

Roundabout

LAKE ONTARIO

Trailhead
Loop Route
Interest Marker
Direction Marker
Conservation Lands

N
W E
S

0    0.12    0.25
Kilometres

"The woods are my religion —
that's why I hike and mountain bike!"

DORI ROSS

*Lake Ontario from Oakville.* PHOTO BY RICHARD OLLEY

# Directions

1. Park in the lot for the Maple Grove Arena at the corner of Elmhurst Ave. and Devon Rd.

2. Look for the Joshua's Valley Park sign and yellow barriers, which lead you down into the shaded valley. Turn right onto the multi-use trail that is popular with dog walkers, runners and cyclists. Cross a footbridge over Joshua's Creek and pass underneath Ford Dr. Already you are leaving the hubbub of city life behind.

3. Veer right at the paved trail intersection just past Ford Dr. and cross another small bridge. We saw some enormous jack-in-the-pulpits here. My dad used to tell me that if I found a jack-in-the-pulpit, he'd give me a dime. I never found one for my dad, so no fortunes made.

4. Veer right again by a post, taking the dirt path.

5. Go up the stairs and turn right onto the paved path. There are houses on your left.

6. Turn left at the next turn and go downhill toward the creek, where the trail turns to dirt and follows alongside Joshua's Creek for a time. Pass by some stairs. Soon after, the main groomed trail climbs away from the creek. Follow it up the bank. Turn left at the top of the bank, keeping the chain-link fence on your right. Behind the fence is the lovely, the beautiful, the spectacular — Oakville wastewater treatment plant.

7. When you come to Lakeshore Rd. E, cross it carefully and enter Arkendo Park via a path on the left side of Arkendo Dr. Joshua's Creek is still on your left and there are houses on your right.

8. When you come to Lake Ontario, look for the big, healthy apple trees and stop to enjoy the view. At one time, apple orchards were common throughout what is now Oakville. Toronto can be seen in the distance to your left. Go right, following a path that runs west along the lakeshore. Note how the air temperature has dropped now that you are by water.

9. On a clear day, you can see buildings on the far side of the lake. I was told it is easier to see them in the evening.

10. Sadly, the trail along the lakeshore ends at the last house in the row. Turn right here, following the trail. The path turns to brick, though not yellow brick.

11. When you come to a street (Arkendo Dr.), veer left and walk up this pretty road until you come to Lakeshore Rd. E, where you turn left.

12. Turn left onto Birkbank Dr., and walk along it until you come to Carrington Pl., where you turn right. Almost immediately turn left onto the footpath (Carrington Promenade) and follow it down to the lakeshore again.

13. At the lakeshore, turn right and walk parallel to the lake. Note all the wonderful homes.

*Trumpeter swans frequent Lake Ontario.*
PHOTO BY RICHARD OLLEY

14. When you come to a little roundabout, turn right.

15. When you return to Carrington Pl., turn right and then go left onto Birkbank Dr.

16. Cross Lakeshore Rd. E again, with caution. Continue straight ahead on the street that is now called Armiger Lane.

17. Armiger Lane comes to a turnaround. Turn left here, onto the driveway into a sports field. Go straight ahead, leaving the driveway, onto the grass between some smallish trees until you come to the sports field. There is a baseball diamond and a soccer pitch.

*The mighty Pathfinders Hiking Group of Oakville.*

Walk alongside the sports field, with the soccer pitch on your left and a swampy forest on your right.

18. Just after a small set of bleachers (hopefully the bleachers don't move), part way along the soccer pitch, turn right onto a path that goes into the trees.

19. At the next intersection of trails, turn left onto the larger shale path. Follow this path as it bears right. The wastewater plant is on your right.

20. Follow the path to the edge of the ravine and turn left, staying on the shoulder of the ravine.

21. Follow the creek (on your right) staying on the shoulder of the ravine. Pass by a wooden fence on your right and continue until you come to the top of a set of stairs.

22. Go down the stairs and keep going straight (leftish). Then stay right.

23. Shortly, the trail climbs out of the valley. At the top of the short rise, make a U-turn to the right and cross over Joshua's Creek.

24. At the next intersection, stay left and go down the wooden stairs, veering left. You climbed these stairs earlier.

25. When you come to the overpass for Ford Dr., turn left and go under the overpass again.

26. Veer left at the next trail intersection, cross the metal bridge, veering left and up the hill. Head back to your car by the Maple Grove Arena.

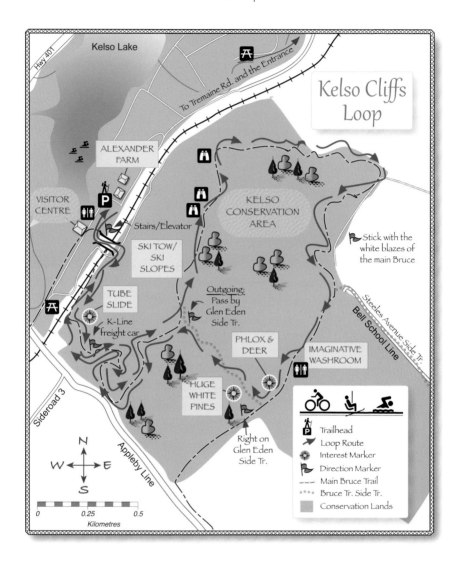

Kelso Cliffs Loop

Kelso Lake

Hwy 401

To Tremaine Rd. and the Entrance

ALEXANDER FARM

VISITOR CENTRE

P

Stairs/Elevator

KELSO CONSERVATION AREA

Stick with the white blazes of the main Bruce

SKI TOW/ SKI SLOPES

Outgoing: Pass by Glen Eden Side Tr.

TUBE SLIDE

K-Line freight car

Steeles Avenue Side Tr.

Bell School Line

PHLOX & DEER

IMAGINATIVE WASHROOM

Sideroad 3

Appleby Line

HUGE WHITE PINES

Right on Glen Eden Side Tr.

Trailhead
Loop Route
Interest Marker
Direction Marker
Main Bruce Trail
Bruce Tr. Side Tr.
Conservation Lands

N
W E
S

0    0.25    0.5
Kilometres

*"Hiking provides a special time to communicate with a family member or good friend as you walk side by side. Now, I have also discovered the numerous benefits of using Nordic walking poles."*

TINA DAALDEROP

# Kelso Cliffs Loop
## (Campbellville)

*There are mountain bike races at Kelso on Tuesday nights, so I'd avoid hiking then. Keep watch for bicycles at all times.* • *Reservations may be required. Make reservation for the main entrance at https://www.conservationhalton.ca.*

## OVERVIEW

I tricked my friend Gail into doing this hike. As we motored along the 401, she couldn't help asking, "Just where are we going?" It didn't help that I took a few wrong turns getting to the trailhead, and then parked the car about a kilometre away from where I suggest you park. But Gail did recognize the lengths I go to, to make your hike more enjoyable by suggesting where to park and how to find the trailhead.

When the helpful woman from Halton Heritage pointed to the cliffs high above, Gail scowled, giving me a look that said, "I would have worn better shoes if you'd mentioned we were climbing a mountain." Fortunately, Gail is a good sport, and this is a fabulous hike. The climb up looks daunting, but we both agreed that it appeared to be 10-times tougher than it is. When we came upon a large, flat rocky outcropping that provided us with a view of rocky cliffs, Kelso Lake, soaring vultures and a vast vista of Ontario farmland, Gail forgave me. Her forgiveness was complete when, after our hike, we stopped at the Flying Monkey Bike Shop & Coffee Bar in Campbellville for a top-notch latte.

> **Conservation Halton**
> (www.conservationhalton.ca) *encourages you and your family to enjoy the trails at all of our parks.*

## 24

### Nicola's
### Insider Info

**LENGTH**
8.7 kilometres

**LEVEL OF DIFFICULTY**
Moderate

**LENGTH OF TIME**
2 to 3 hours

**NUMBER OF STEPS**
12,454

**kCAL BURNED** 377

**HIGHLIGHTS**
Cliffs, Alexander farm, mix of forest and fields, views, elevator!

**PLACES TO EAT/DRINK**
Flying Monkey Bike Shop & Coffee Bar and The Trail Eatery in Campbellville

**ENTRANCE FEE**
Adult $9.50/Senior (65+) $7.50/Child (5–14) $6.50/ Child (<5) free

**HOURS**
Park opens 8:30am daily.

**TRAILHEAD**
N43° 30.258' W79° 56.782'

**BRUCE TRAIL MAP** 11

**TRAIL MARKER**
*Loop 24*

## Directions

1. Park in the Kelso Conservation Area via the main entrance. It's on Kelso Rd., off Tremaine Rd., south of Hwy. 401. Park close to what appears to be an odd-looking building (but is actually covered stairs and an elevator that go over the railway tracks).

2. Before heading out on the trail, I suggest you wander around what used to be the Alexander family farm. Adam Alexander III owned it until 1941. An ingenious man, he tapped the water power of the Niagara Escarpment, piping water to a turbine in his barn. There, he fitted it so it supplied a water fountain (there are remains), a washing machine and a number of other "modern conveniences." He even rigged it with a "dynamo," which resulted in his family having electricity long before it otherwise became available. Imagine if Adam Alexander III ran Ontario Hydro.

3. After a wander past the old stone house, log house, blacksmith shop and pond, head back to the stairs by the fenced-off railway tracks. There are even 2, count 'em, 2, elevators here. Pick up the white blazes of the main Bruce Tr.

4. On the other side of the tracks, turn right and head back down toward the railway tracks. Turn left and follow the white blazes alongside the tracks.

*I recommend visiting the Alexander farm.*

*A view well worth the climb.*

5. Pass behind a tube slide and turn left, heading uphill toward a K-Line shipping container.

6. The trail goes to the right of the container and enters the forest. Go right on the main Bruce Tr. with its white blazes and begin climbing. There are signs directing you toward the lime kiln, and the Bruce Tr. follows the Lime Kiln Tr., but summer foliage can obscure the old ruin, plus it is "craftily" hidden behind a wire-mesh fence with a helpful sign that warns "Danger. Keep Out. No Trespassing."

7. For the next 5k you follow the white blazes of the main Bruce Tr. Lots of other trails cross the path, but stick to the main Bruce Tr. Not only will this ensure you don't end up walking on a trail designated for mountain bikes, but the main Bruce Tr. is the most picturesque route. So when you come to an intersection of trails, just look for the next white blaze.

8. The trail follows the vertical cliff face that looks north. You may have noticed this ridge as you drive along the 401. There are a number of lookout points along here. Try them all out, though our favourite was one that is just after the one at the top of a chairlift. It comes out onto a flat rocky surface, and you can see cliffs to your right and a wonderful vista of farmland beyond

*I still don't know what this place is!*

Kelso Lake. The vultures soared below us and we felt pretty pleased that we'd made the climb up. This is a great place to stop for photos, snacks or lunch.

9. The trail passes through an elegant hardwood forest with signature Niagara Escarpment rocky outcrops and fissures. Then it opens onto farm fields and meadows. Stay with the main Bruce Tr.'s white blazes. I particularly loved the washroom along a trail named Old Farm Lane. See for yourself. There must have been a farm here once and it's neat to see how the forest is regenerating. This is where we saw a deer amid vibrant phlox.

10. At one point, we looked from the forest, across an open meadow to a distant lake. I snapped a photo of a number of colourful buildings on the far side.

11. Along the way, you come twice to the Bruce Tr.'s Glen Eden Side Tr. with blue blazes. The 1st time, it heads off to your right. DO NOT take it. When you see it again, an hour or so later, it goes right again. This time you will take it, finally leaving the white blazes.

12. Follow the Glen Eden Side Tr. for its entire length (700m). When it ends, turn left and pick up the white blazes of the main Bruce Tr. again.

13. I contemplated taking one of the other trails down to avoid retracing our footsteps, but some of them are cycle-only, and they are not as nice as the Bruce Tr. So stick with the white blazes.

14. You come out of the forest and pass by the K-Line container en route to the building with the stairs and elevator and your car.

# Limehouse Combo Loop

*In this loop, I direct you to walk along a 125m portion of the Brown Benton Side Trail that links 4th Line to the Canada Goose Side Trail. Although the Brown Benton Side Trail is currently closed, the Bruce Trail Conservancy says this 125m portion of the trail will remain open year-round.*

## OVERVIEW

There is no particular destination on this loop. No lookout or ruins or waterfall. But you go a long way without having to worry about roads or houses. You also walk through forest and across farmland, which is a great mix, in my opinion. Some of the nicest trail is just before you reach 4th Line. It passes through a mature forest and by a pond that is favoured by muskrats. Muskrats build dwelling houses, such as the one in the pond on this route, and smaller feeding houses.

When you are enjoying this hike, remember that most of the routes in this guide are within the 720,000-hectare Ontario Greenbelt (**www.greenbelt.ca**), which is the world's largest permanently protected greenbelt and consists of farmland, forests and wetlands. Check out the Greenbelt Routes offered by the Greenbelt Foundation. (**www.greenbelt.ca/route**)

*Hiking through forests and across farmland is just one of many activities to take advantage of in Ontario's Greenbelt. (**www.greenbelt.ca**)*

## Nicola's
## Insider Info

**LENGTH**
11.5 kilometres

**LEVEL OF DIFFICULTY**
Easy

**LENGTH OF TIME**
3 to 4 hours

**NUMBER OF STEPS**
15,299

**kCAL BURNED** 615

**HIGHLIGHTS**
Long forested stretches, muskrat home

**PLACES TO EAT/DRINK**
Heather's Bakery, Silvercreek Socialhaus, The St. George Pub, Symposium Café Restaurant & Lounge in Georgetown/Kit's Little Kitchen, The Glen Tavern, Copper Kettle Pub in Glen Williams

**ENTRANCE FEE**
n/a

**TRAILHEAD**
N43° 37.548'W79° 59.449'

**BRUCE TRAIL MAP** 12

TRAIL MARKER
*Loop 25*

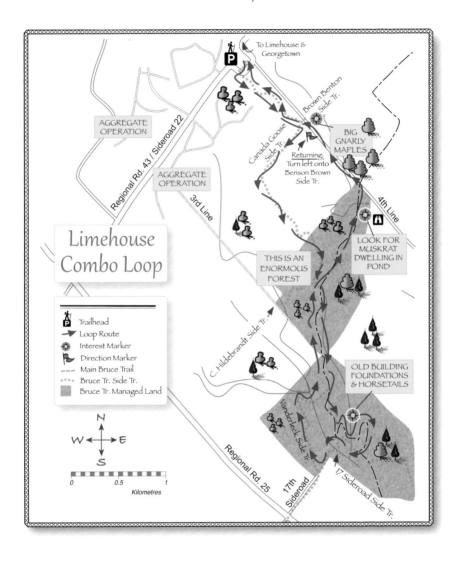

To Limehouse & Georgetown

Brown Benton Side Tr.

AGGREGATE OPERATION

Regional Rd. 43 / Sideroad 22

Canada Goose Side Tr.

BIG GNARLY MAPLES

Returning: Turn left onto Benson Brown Side Tr.

AGGREGATE OPERATION

3rd Line

4th Line

LOOK FOR MUSKRAT DWELLING IN POND

## Limehouse Combo Loop

THIS IS AN ENORMOUS FOREST

C. Hildebrandt Side Tr.

OLD BUILDING FOUNDATIONS & HORSETAILS

**Trailhead**
Loop Route
Interest Marker
Direction Marker
Main Bruce Trail
Bruce Tr. Side Tr.
Bruce Tr. Managed Land

N
W — E
S

Vanderleck Side Tr.

Regional Rd. 25

17th Sideroad

17 Sideroad Side Tr.

0       0.5       1
Kilometres

*Hiking in the forest feels like a renewal
or a reset for me each weekend.*

CAROL SHEPPARD

*Pause to enjoy these wetlands.*

# Directions

1. Park in the Bruce Tr. parking lot on 22 Sideroad, just west of the 4th Line Halton Hills, about 2k west of Limehouse. It's hidden, but you will find it.

2. Walk out of the parking lot and turn right onto Sideroad 22. Turn left onto the Canada Goose Side Tr. with its blue blazes (about 100m from the parking lot).

3. You enter an area with rocky outcroppings and some big gnarled maples on your right.

4. At the intersection with the Brown Benton Side Tr., stay right and continue on the Canada Goose Side Tr.

5. The trail travels close to some fields that open onto aggregate pits. I'm not a fan of these pits, but liked that a little sunshine hit the trail in this section.

6. Climb another stile and pass by the Charles Hildebrandt Side Tr., which was named after a valued volunteer with the Bruce Tr.'s Toronto Club.

7. At the end of the Canada Goose Side Tr., turn right and follow the white blazes of the main Bruce Tr.

8. You go through an enormous forest. Some of it is quite wild, while other sections seemed to be tightly managed and have almost no undergrowth and all similar-sized trees.

*Limestone rocks are seldom in short supply
on the Niagara Escarpment.* PHOTO BY SHIRLEY WHITE

9.  Pass by the Vanderleck Side Tr., staying on the main Bruce Tr. with its white blazes.

10. Look for the crumbling foundations of what might have been old farm buildings. Keep your eyes peeled for cultivated flowers that have gone wild. At these old farmsteads, it's common to find hollyhocks, oriental poppies, ground phlox or possibly chives that are left over from times gone by.

11. Soon, you come across some green plants that look like miniature bamboo. These horsetail ferns are the solo member of their genus and are ancient plants dating back to the dinosaurs.

12. Leave the main Bruce Tr., turning right onto the 17 Sideroad Side Tr. with its blue blazes. Follow this side trail until it ends at the easterly end of 17th Sideroad, bypassing several logging roads.

13. Turn right here, picking up the blue blazes marking the Vanderleck Side Tr. and re-enter the forest.

14. The Vanderleck Side Tr. ends at the next trail intersection. Turn left here and follow the white blazes of the main Bruce Tr.

15. Pass by the Canada Goose Side Tr.

16. The trail drops down and, foliage allowing, you can see through the trees to a vista beyond. The sun was streaming over my shoulder at one point, and I got a lovely photo of the path that seemed to have a light shining from within.

17. Stop at the pond and look for the rounded mound in the centre. Made from cattails and other soft materials, it's the dwelling house for some muskrats. If you have time, take a seat by the pond and see if these clever, albeit primarily nocturnal, animals make an appearance. In archaic English, muskrats were called "musquash." More recently, they have been called "musk beavers" because they mark their territory with a musk-like compound and have some other similarities to their larger cousins. Both are rodents with impressive front teeth. Muskrats have been known to cohabit in a beaver lodge, and while some scientists claim they eat young beavers, other observers suggest they actually help feed them.

18. When you arrive at 4th Line, turn left and follow it for about 1k until you see signs for the Bruce Tr. on the left side of the road. Don't miss the blue blazes marking the short Brown Benton Side Tr.

19. Turn left and enter the forest following this path with its blue blazes.

20. After a short 100m, turn right onto the Canada Goose Side Tr. and follow it back to your car.

*Muskrat dwellings are made of softer materials than those used by beavers.*

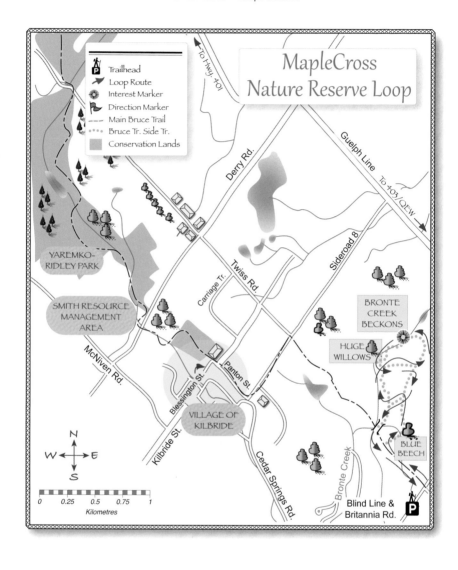

# MapleCross Nature Reserve Loop

**Legend:**
- Trailhead
- Loop Route
- Interest Marker
- Direction Marker
- Main Bruce Trail
- Bruce Tr. Side Tr.
- Conservation Lands

YAREMKO-RIDLEY PARK

SMITH RESOURCE MANAGEMENT AREA

VILLAGE OF KILBRIDE

BRONTE CREEK BECKONS

HUGE WILLOWS

BLUE BEECH

To Hwy. 401

Derry Rd.

Guelph Line

To 403/QEW

Sideroad 8

Twiss Rd.

Carriage Tr.

McNiven Rd.

Blessington St.

Panton St.

Kilbride St.

Cedar Springs Rd.

Bronte Creek

Blind Line & Britannia Rd.

N W E S

0   0.25   0.5   0.75   1
Kilometres

*"What is it about the forest
That makes us feel sublime?
I can feel it in its carpet
That strokes these feet of mine."*

ALEX STRACHAN

# MapleCross
# Nature Reserve Loop
## (Campbellville/Kilbride)

## OVERVIEW

This pretty double lolli-loop route replaces the 15k Yaremko-Ridley Park/Lovely Creek Loop from the original version of Halton Hikes. Changes to the Bruce Trail meant that route would follow too much road and would miss the pretty village of Kilbride. (If you want to see the hamlet, you can drive there after your hike.)

The Iroquoia Bruce Trail Club added two side trails to the River & Ruin Side Trail, making this a lovely route on its own, in large part because you follow Bronte Creek for much of the way. Bronte Creek is cool enough to support cold-water-loving trout. On a hot day, I suggest sitting on the riverbank and dipping your tired feet into the clear stream as you eat a snack or lunch. Consider it Hiker Dodie's orders!

There is an information board along the way that tells you a bit about the MapleCross Nature Reserve at River & Ruin and about Squire Clever and the ruins of the house he built.

*Red trilliums are also known as stinking Benjamin.*

*Fiddleheads*

ABOVE PHOTOS BY MARY TAYLOR

# Directions

1. Park at the intersection of Blind Line and Britannia Rd., where there's a designated area.

2. Follow the white blazes of the main Bruce Tr. as it goes north into the forest at the foot of Blind Line.

3. About 500m later, you come to an intersection of trails. Turn right and follow the blue blazes of the River & Ruin Side Tr. Look for a couple of blue beech trees (*Carpinus caroliniana*) that are on either side of the trail (N43° 25.313′ W79° 54.821′). They are also known as musclewood trees because the smooth ridges on their trunks make them look like muscles. Blue beech is very hard and was used to make axe handles.

4. You will follow a sort of double lolli-loop route as you crisscross back and forth between sections of the River & Ruins Side Tr., following 2 other side trails. Look at the map if the directions sound confusing.

5. You pass through the MapleCross Nature Reserve at River & Ruin along this section of trail. Along the way, you will find the ruins of an old house built by John Clever in the early 1800s. Clever owned the local grist mill,

*Squire Clever's ruins.* PHOTO BY MARY TAYLOR

and was a teacher and surveyor who presumably went by Squire Clever, given the name of one of the side trails.

6. Follow Bronte Creek along this delightful stretch of trail with its quintessential babbling brook. When I was there, masses of ferns and phlox amid enormous willow trees kept me company. Stop alongside the river to forget about the world. There is also an interesting stile made from an old stump.

7. In 300m, turn left onto the Dan Walsh Side Tr., following it until you return to the River & Ruins Side Tr. where you turn right.

8. At the Squire Clever Side Tr., turn right and follow it until you return to the River & Ruins Side Tr., where you turn left.

9. Follow the River & Ruins Side Tr. for about 1k until you come to the Squire Clever Side Tr. again. Turn left here and follow it back to the River & Ruins Side Tr. where you turn right.

10. Follow the River & Ruins Side Tr. back to the Dan Walsh Side Tr. where you turn right. Follow the Dan Walsh Side Tr. back to the River & Ruins Side Tr., where you turn left.

11. Follow the River & Ruins Side Tr. back to the main Bruce Tr.

12. Turn left onto the main Bruce Tr. and follow its white blazes back to Britannia Rd., where your car is parked.

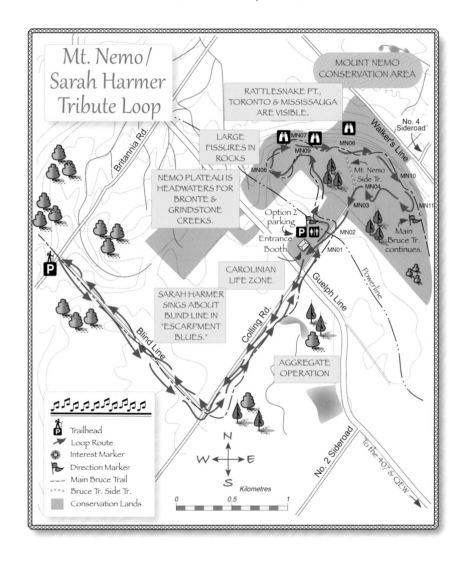

## Mt. Nemo / Sarah Harmer Tribute Loop

MOUNT NEMO CONSERVATION AREA

RATTLESNAKE PT., TORONTO & MISSISSAUGA ARE VISIBLE.

LARGE FISSURES IN ROCKS

NEMO PLATEAU IS HEADWATERS FOR BRONTE & GRINDSTONE CREEKS.

No. 4 Sideroad

Walker's Line

Britannia Rd.

MN07
MN09
MN06
MN08
Mt. Nemo Side Tr.
MN04
MN10
MN03
MN11
MN02
Main Bruce Tr. continues.
MN01

Option 2 parking

Entrance Booth

Powerline

CAROLINIAN LIFE ZONE

SARAH HARMER SINGS ABOUT BLIND LINE IN "ESCARPMENT BLUES."

Blind Line

Colling Rd.

Guelph Line

AGGREGATE OPERATION

No. 2 Sideroad

To the 407 & QEW

**Legend**

- Trailhead
- Loop Route
- Interest Marker
- Direction Marker
- Main Bruce Trail
- Bruce Tr. Side Tr.
- Conservation Lands

N
W E
S

Kilometres

0        0.5        1

*"What's not to hike?"*

NEIL BIRD

# Mt. Nemo/Sarah Harmer Tribute Loop (Lowville)

*You may require a reservation to visit the Mount Nemo Conservation Area. Check at www.conservationhalton.ca.*

## OVERVIEW

This lovely loop has some amazing views of country and city alike from atop Mt. Nemo. The surprisingly gentle climb up passes through a beautiful forest, and then you follow a trail over typical escarpment rocks.

I'm a Sarah Harmer fan. This singer-songwriter grew up close to Mt. Nemo, and the landscape inspires her artistry. To raise awareness about her beloved Niagara Escarpment, she went on an "I Love the Escarpment" tour in 2005. With her band, she walked the Bruce Trail and played concerts along the way, raising funds and talking about protecting the escarpment from aggregate development. I attended the concert in tiny Mono Centre, north of Orangeville. It was a memorable, rocking night. Harmer turned the tour into a documentary film called *Escarpment Blues*, and it won the 2007 Juno Award for Best Music DVD. In the song, she sings about "driving on the Blind Line." The tribute part of this loop is the walk along that very road. Call me a Sarah Harmer groupie, but I thought this was a way that I could thank a fellow Niagara Escarpment–lover for her activism.

> **Conservation Halton**
> (www.conservationhalton.ca) *encourages you and your family to enjoy the trails at all of our parks.*

**27**

## Nicola's Insider Info

**LENGTH**
12.4 kilometres
(5.3k option)

**LEVEL OF DIFFICULTY**
Moderate

**LENGTH OF TIME**
3 to 4 hours
(1.5 to 2 hours)

**NUMBER OF STEPS**
16,304

**kCAL BURNED**  675

**HIGHLIGHTS**
Views, views, views, rock climbing

**PLACES TO EAT/DRINK**
Flying Monkey Bike Shop & Coffee Bar, The Trail Eatery in Campbellville/ Lowville Bistro in Lowville

**ENTRANCE FEE**
Adult $9.50/Senior (65+) $7.50/Child (5–14) $6.50/ Child (<5) free

**HOURS**
Park opens at 8:30am daily

**TRAILHEAD**
N43° 25.033'W79° 54.670'
(N43° 25.025'W79° 52.917')

**BRUCE TRAIL MAP**  10

**TRAIL MARKER**
*Loop 27*

# Directions

## Longer Option (12.4k total hike)

1. Park in the designated area at the intersection of Blind Line and Britannia Rd. It's south of Hwy. 401.

2. Walk south on Blind Line up the hill, following the white blazes of the main Bruce Tr. (DO NOT go into the forest here.)

3. Some 2k in length, Blind Line isn't particularly remarkable, so I hummed Sarah Harmer's "Escarpment Blues," pleased that her efforts and those of the entire team known as PERL (Protecting Escarpment Rural Lands) had successfully fought against the Mt. Nemo quarry. Though in 2021 there was a new application to expand the pit she opposed.

4. When you come to Colling Rd, cross it and a small wooden bridge. The main Bruce Tr. turns left and runs parallel to Colling Rd, and so do you. As the pair who tested this hike for me suggested, nature is battling back after being decimated by aggregate development along here. Hardy dogwood, milkweed, staghorn sumac and wild grapes are gaining a foothold.

5. At Guelph Line, cross this busy road carefully and enter the Mt. Nemo Conservation Area. If you have a Bruce Tr. or a Halton Parks membership and your card in hand, there is no charge.

6. Walk past the entrance booth and a metal barrier. The washroom situated here is well maintained. When you come to an information sign at post MN01, stop to learn more about Mt. Nemo.

7. As the story goes, Nemo, which means "nobody" in Latin, received its name after authorities couldn't think of what else to call a nearby post office.

8. Continue up the road. Turn left at post MN02, following the white blazes of the main Bruce Tr. as it leaves the road and enters a treed area. Stick with the main Bruce Tr. for the next 3k.

9. Bypass MN09, MN08 and MN07, as you make your way around the top of Mt. Nemo. There are spectacular views across

*This is what I call a "bird's eye" view.*
PHOTO BY ANNE CROWE

a vast patchwork of farm fields and big horse farms. Behind them, the Niagara Escarpment rises again at Rattlesnake Point. The trail here is rocky with lots of fissures to explore. I came across a couple of rock climbers and got to see them rappel down the near-vertical cliff. As you round Mt. Nemo, the city of Mississauga

*One of many vistas along this loop.*
PHOTO BY ANNE CROWE

comes into view and then a little further along, you can see the CN Tower in Toronto. I snapped a photo that makes it look as if Mississauga and Toronto are one enormous megacity. That made me wonder if this was the future.

10. At post MN06, stop for the spectacular view from the Brock Harris Lookout. Then continue straight, continuing to follow the white blazes of main Bruce Tr. This is also the start of the South Loop Tr. It has yellow markers.

11. Follow this trail through a short stretch of deep forest that opens up into less dense vegetation.

12. Bypass MB10. At MB11, turn right leaving the main Bruce Tr. and its white blazes. Continue following the yellow markers for the South Loop Tr.

13. At MN04, go left, still following the South Loop Tr.

14. At MN03, the South Loop Tr. ends. Turn left here onto the Mt. Nemo Side Tr., following its blue blazes back to the entrance booth.

15. Continue out of the conservation area. At Guelph Line, turn left.

16. Retrace the route along Colling Rd., and then go right onto Blind Line for a 2nd chance to salute Harmer and her colleagues at PERL.

17. When you come to the end of Blind Line, presumably so named because it dead-ends at each end, you will have returned to your car.

## Shorter Option (5.3k total hike)

1. Park in the lot at the Mt. Nemo Conservation Area.

2. Follow Points #6 to #14 above.

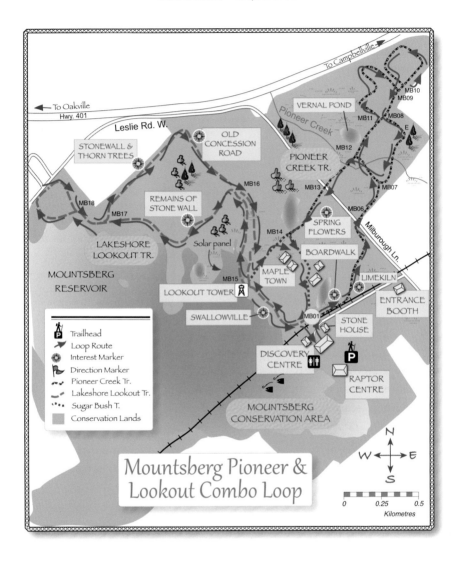

Mountsberg Pioneer & Lookout Combo Loop

*"I hike so I can see things beneath the concrete sidewalk and truly experience the world beyond the car window!"*

SUSAN GESNER

# Mountsberg Pioneer & Lookout Combo Loop
## (Campbellville)

*You may require a reservation to visit the Mountsberg Conservation Area. Check at www.conservationhalton.ca. These loops can be muddy, wet and buggy in the spring.*

## OVERVIEW

This pair of hikes is located entirely within the Mountsberg Conservation Area near Campbellville. They can be done as a single 3- to 5-hour loop or separately as 2 distinct 1.5- to 2.5-hour loops. If you only hike one of them, I'd suggest the 6.5k Pioneer Creek Trail.

The Mountsberg Conservation Area is best known for what it offers to families with children. There's an amazing raptor centre (home for birds unable to survive in the wild), a wildlife walkway and barns where kids can play on hay bales. Maple Town is a full-scale syrup-making operation, and you can fish. This means it can be besieged by screeching youngsters, delighted by a great horned owl, a red-tailed hawk or a spill in a haymow. Keep this in mind if you want peaceful hiking. Similarly, Highway 401 borders the conservation area, and you are never entirely out of sound range on what are pleasant, if not particularly interesting, routes. This description won't sell all hikers on these loops, but if you have kids, like the idea of getting "beak-to-lens" with raptors or think it's high time for a lakeshore picnic, go for it.

## Nicola's
## Insider Info

**LENGTH**
14 kilometres or as separate 6.5k & 7.5k loops

**LEVEL OF DIFFICULTY**
Easy

**LENGTH OF TIME**
3 to 5 hours
(1.5 to 2.5 hours per loop)

**NUMBER OF STEPS**
18,041

**kCAL BURNED**  699

**HIGHLIGHTS**
Swallowville, Mountsberg Reservoir, raptor centre, wildlife walkway, barns, Maple Town, Discovery Centre, fishing

**PLACES TO EAT/DRINK**
Discovery Centre (light snacks only)/Flying Monkey Bike Shop & Coffee Bar, The Trail Eatery in Campbellville/ Lowville Bistro in Lowville

**ENTRANCE FEE**
Adult $9.50/Senior (65+) $7.50/ Child (5–14) $6.50/ Child (<5) free

**HOURS**
Summer: 8:30am–9pm

**TRAILHEAD**
N43° 27.597'W80° 01.823'

**BRUCE TRAIL MAP**  10

GPS

**TRAIL MARKER**
*Loop 28*

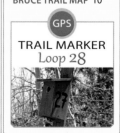

# Directions

1. Park in the area provided by the Mountsberg Conservation Area.

2. From the parking area, walk toward the Discovery Centre and either pass through it or walk around to the other side where there are trail signs. Walk by the 1st barn on your left and then turn right between the railway tracks and the lovely stone house that is on your right.

3. Turn left and cross the tracks via a gate marked "Caution" and walk straight on.

4. Ahead of you is the trailhead sign and post MB01. Turn right here, following the orange markers for the 6.5k Pioneer Creek Tr. (PCT) along a boardwalk that spans a wetland, alive with the sounds of birds and bullfrogs.

5. A short 300m later, there is a sign for a lime kiln. Limestone was cooked in this small, round structure to produce lime, which was used as mortar and to produce soap.

6. Stay on the PCT as it emerges from the forest and parallels, then crosses, paved Millborough Line. Bypass MB06. At MB07, turn left following the Pioneer Creek Shortcut, crossing Pioneer Creek. At MB12, turn right.

7. Pass by a pond on your left, turn left at MB11 and follow the trail around Pioneer Creek Loop 1, returning to the main trail at MB09. Look for an old stone chimney on the loop.

8. Upon returning to the main trail, turn left. Continue past MB10 around Pioneer Creek Loop 2. Parts of these smaller loops can be muddy and buggy, depending on the season and the weather.

9. When you return to the main trail at MB10, turn right and follow the main trail past MB09 to MB08, where you turn left.

*This is what remains of a small lime kiln.*

*The Mountsberg Reservoir reportedly has superb largemouth bass fishing.*
PHOTO BY RICHARD OLLEY

10. Cross a small stream and stay left at an old signpost E. There is a lovely big spruce tree here. Stay right and cross a wooden bridge over Pioneer Cr.

11. Turn right at MB07, once again following the Pioneer Creek Shortcut.

12. At MB12, turn left following the PCT back toward the Discovery Centre. Cross the paved road again and bypass MB13.

13. This straight section of trail follows an old road, and it was my favourite part of the hike when I first walked this route. I was there in late April, and the forest was overflowing with trilliums, bloodroot and blue cohosh. Marsh marigolds were about to pop open. Spring was everywhere.

14. Continue down the road until you come to MB14, where you turn left to enter Maple Town. In March and early April, it would be fun to see the "town" in full operation. In the Discovery Centre, they sell maple syrup and other maple products made here.

15. Head toward the wooden buildings, following the road that passes between them. The road veers right and you stay on it. Pass under the overhead sign that reads "Thank you for visiting."

16. Further up the road is the trailhead sign at MB01.

*Now you have a decision to make. Do you want to keep hiking or explore the other things the Mountsberg Conservation Area has to offer?*

## Longer Option (14k total hike)

17. Go straight, passing the trailhead sign at MB01 and picking up the occasional blue markers for the 7.5k Lakeshore Lookout Tr.

18. Walking along a small road, you come to Swallowville, a collection of birdhouses that was alive with iridescent tree swallows when I was there. Some were perched on their homes in the warm sunshine, while others swooped, catching mouthfuls of insects. Swallowville was a highlight for me.

19. Continue following the road until you come to a trail intersection with the Sugar Bush Loop at post MB15. Turn left here to visit a lookout tower with a nice view of the enormous Mountsberg Reservoir. After a look-see, return to the road at post MB15, where you turn left and continue along the Lakeshore Lookout Tr.

20. You pass by a picnic table before arriving at a trail sign where you veer left. Stay on the road past a laneway leading to some maintenance sheds, and then look for a big old oak tree on your right.

21. At post MB16, turn left, leaving the road to follow a grassy path. The reservoir is visible through the trees to your left.

22. At the T-intersection turn left, passing by some old birdhouses.

23. At post MB17, turn left and then look for a small side-path down to the reservoir past a huge "swamp" willow.

24. At MB18 turn left.

*Tree swallows in their glory.*

25. Keep following the mown path as it goes in a ring around a reforested area. For one stretch you'll walk parallel to Leslie Rd. W. Just after the trail turns right and leaves Leslie Rd. W., look to your left for some beautiful old maples.

26. When you return to MB18, go straight. A sign says there is a "steep" hill. I'd call it gentle.

27. At MB17 stay left. Note the old stone fence to your left. It's hidden by some hawthorn trees. Together, the wall and thorny trees would have made a good line of defense for livestock.

*I know these iris don't look real, but they are!* PHOTO BY RICHARD OLLEY

28. At a post with no number on it (when I hiked it), turn right. I'm pretty sure this is the old concession road.

29. Staying on the fairly well-worn path, bypass a mown path to your right before passing by a laneway that leads to a beautiful old stone house. Completing the ring, you come to MB16 where you turned left earlier. Continue straight ahead.

30. When you return to post MB15, turn left onto the Sugar Bush Loop, along a very straight road lined on both sides by an extensive swamp.

31. At post MB14, turn right, following the Sugar Bush Loop and its red markers toward Maple Town: a maple sugar operation.

32. Pass to the left of the buildings until you see the double red doors and a washroom sign on a building where you turn right, leaving Maple Town under a large sign that reads: "Thank you for joining us!"

33. Up ahead you will see the gates at the railway tracks. Cross over the tracks carefully, turn right to pass by the beautiful stone house. Turn left toward the Discovery Centre and return to the parking lot and your vehicle.

## Shorter Option (6.5k total hike)

1. Continued from Point #16.

2. Return to the Discovery Centre and your car by carefully crossing the railway tracks again and retracing your footsteps.

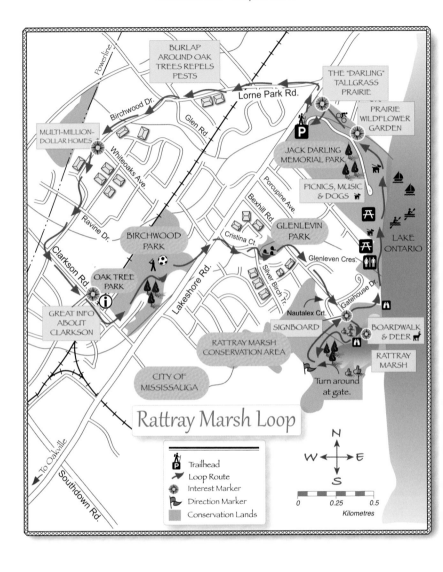

**Rattray Marsh Loop**

BURLAP AROUND OAK TREES REPELS PESTS

THE "DARLING" TALLGRASS PRAIRIE

PRAIRIE WILDFLOWER GARDEN

Powerline

Lorne Park Rd.

Birchwood Dr.

Glen Rd.

JACK DARLING MEMORIAL PARK

MULTI-MILLION-DOLLAR HOMES

Whiteoaks Ave.

PICNICS, MUSIC & DOGS

Porcupine Ave.

LAKE ONTARIO

Ravine Dr.

Bexhill Rd.

Cristina Ct.

GLENLEVIN PARK

BIRCHWOOD PARK

Clarkson Rd.

Glenleven Cres.

OAK TREE PARK

Lakeshore Rd.

Silver Birch Tr.

Gatehouse Dr.

GREAT INFO ABOUT CLARKSON

Nautalex Crt.

BOARDWALK & DEER

SIGNBOARD

RATTRAY MARSH

RATTRAY MARSH CONSERVATION AREA

CITY OF MISSISSAUGA

Turn around at gate.

To Oakville

Southdown Rd.

**Legend**

🅿 Trailhead

Loop Route

Interest Marker

Direction Marker

Conservation Lands

N W E S

0    0.25    0.5
Kilometres

*"Hiking brings me peace, grounding and back to nature.
It's something that almost everyone can do.
And the cost is next to nil."*

RENEE HOLDEN

# Rattray Marsh Loop
(Mississauga)

## OVERVIEW

Located in Mississauga, just over the border from Halton, the Rattray Marsh is the last "baymouth bar," coastal marsh on the western end of Lake Ontario. It has been designated as a Natural Area, a Provincially Significant Wetland and an Area of Natural and Scientific Interest. Some 38ha in size, the Rattray Marsh Conservation Area is tucked away — an oasis within one of Canada's largest cities. Credit Valley Conservation and a group of local citizens have taken great pride in building walkways that get you right into the marsh.

I walked through it at noon on a hot Sunday that was also Father's Day. Despite the heat, I watched a lovely white-tailed buck for about 10 minutes. He was quite content to have me observe him at my leisure — and his. The Rattray Marsh is also the place to learn about the emerald ash borer, as almost half of the property was covered in ash trees, all of which are dying as a result of this pest. The loop connects Rattray Marsh to Jack Darling Memorial Park along the Waterfront Trail. You see tallgrass prairie and prairie gardens before walking along some very fine streets in Lorne Park.

## Nicola's Insider Info

**LENGTH**
8.8 kilometres

**LEVEL OF DIFFICULTY**
Easy

**LENGTH OF TIME**
2 to 3 hours

**NUMBER OF STEPS**
11,671

**kCAL BURNED** 354

**HIGHLIGHTS**
Buck deer, size of the wetland, boardwalks, waterfront, prairie gardens, Oak Tree Park

**PLACES TO EAT/DRINK**
The Apricot Tree Café, Capra's Kitchen, Symposium Café Restaurant & Lounge in Mississauga

**ENTRANCE FEE**
There is a donation box by the signage for the Rattray Marsh.

**TRAILHEAD**
There are 5 parking lots in Jack Darling Park. All are free, but busy.

**TRAILHEAD**
N43° 31.798' W79° 36.512'

## TRAIL MARKER
Loop 29

# Directions

1. From whichever of Jack Darling Park's 5 parking lots, make your way to Lakeshore Rd. W. Turn right onto Lakeshore Rd. W. and follow it to the traffic lights at Lorne Park Rd. Cross here and follow Lorne Park Rd. all the way to Birchwood Dr. (about 1k). Walking along these streets isn't the best. As you'll see, though, it closes a wonderful loop.

2. Enjoy this tony neighbourhood. In the area near Whiteoaks Ave. there are some eye-catching houses.

3. At Birchwood Dr., turn left, making sure you pick up Birchwood and NOT Glen Rd.

4. Birchwood snakes its way for 1.4k all the way to Clarkson Rd. N. At intersections make sure you stay on Birchwood.

5. Turn left onto Clarkson Rd. N, heading toward the lake. Keep your eyes peeled for tiny Oak Tree Park on your left. It is home to an enormous, centuries-old oak tree. Read the signs about how Clarkson came to be.

6. Cross the railway tracks and pass by the sign for Birchwood Park on your left. Just before houses start again, turn left into the park, along a vague grassy path, with a fence on your right and a parking lot on your left. The path soon becomes paved. Pass by a soccer field and a few baseball diamonds. The path bends to the right, heading back toward Lake Ontario.

7. The trail spills out onto Lakeshore Rd. W, where you turn left. Cross Lakeshore Rd. W at the traffic lights at Johnson's Lane, and turn left, still heading east on Lakeshore Rd. W. When you come to a few small spruce trees and a paved sidewalk that veers away from Lakeshore Rd. W, follow it through an opening in a metal fence. Take this diagonal sidewalk down onto Cristina Crt.

*This white-tailed buck seemed more curious than fearful. I guess that's life for deer in the city.*

8. Cross the street and continue along the sidewalk. It bends sharply to the right and then the left.

*It's an enormous marsh, and it's right in Mississauga.*

9. At Silver Birch Tr., turn right, cross the street and then turn left into little Glenleven Park near the wood fence at the far end of the park. There is a vague grassy trail that disappears, so keep walking on the grass. There are some birch trees and a creek on your left and a fence on your right.

10. At Bexhill Rd., turn right and follow it past Gatehouse Dr. and into the Rattray Marsh Conservation Area.

11. Walk down the slope to the signboard, where there is a donation box and a map of the trails within the marsh. Go past the signboard, straight ahead toward the lake and pick up an unmarked trail that veers to the right and has railings on either side. This is the Knoll Tr.

12. Enter the shady forest, carpeted with ferns and mayapples, and pick up the boardwalk as you near the marsh. There are great views, so take your time and look for some of the 200 species of birds that visit and/or live in the Rattray Marsh.

13. The trail loops back, and you come to an intersection where you turn left onto the Pedestrian Waterfront Tr. This is where I spent a good 10 minutes watching a white-tailed buck. He wasn't the least bit skittish and, in fact, seemed to stare me down. Whereas deer in rural areas are afraid of humans who sometimes have guns, he was quite happy to have a drink of water and let me snap a few photos.

*Father's Day.*

14. Follow this trail until signage says the Waterfront Tr. turns left and there is small metal gate up ahead. Turn around at this point and begin retracing your route in. Pass by the Knoll Tr., walking straight ahead on the Pedestrian Waterfront Tr. Pass the signboard and donation box.

15. Veer right onto the boardwalk and path that leads to Lake Ontario. There are some well-placed logs to sit on and a shore full of flat skipping stones. I watched a kayaker glide by, some terns intent on finding lunch in the water and several sailboats. I gazed down the shoreline at what appeared to be complete wilderness, and then turned to look the other way where Toronto's impressive skyline was almost in my lap.

16. Return to the Pedestrian Waterfront Tr. and turn right, continuing with Lake Ontario on your right. The trail leaves the Rattray Marsh, hugging the shoreline until you enter Jack Darling Memorial Park. There are washrooms and picnic tables in this area.

17. As it was Father's Day, 32°C and sunny, the park was alive with families. Barbecues were hot, reggae music rocked, and a dog's breakfast of dogs competed for sticks thrown into the lake. This route is definitely an urban one. It was fun to see all the life and energy and people.

18. The trail bends left, leaving the lakefront. Pass by the Prairie Wildflower Garden and then the "Darling" Tallgrass Prairie, both of which are described on signboards, before you approach Lakeshore Rd. W. Stay left on this multi-use path.

19. Return to your vehicle.

# Rockwood Pothole Loop

## OVERVIEW

I hiked this loop on a Sunday afternoon in mid-April. It was 24°C and sunny. The warm spring sun on my back felt so good that any route would have been a pleasure, but this is a gem. It reminded me of one of those two-bite brownies: small, but full of flavour.

Rockwood is situated on the Eramosa River, a tributary to the Grand. The Eramosa was sufficiently powerful that it attracted early settlers, who built, among other things, a woolen mill, the spectacular ruins of which are en route. The Eramosa broadens out within the Rockwood Conservation Area, forming a small lake that is dotted with limestone islands. When I was there, families were canoeing and kayaking. The Pothole Trail, so named because there are more than 200 "potholes" in the area, was fascinating. The potholes were formed by water when the Wisconsin Glacier receded some 11,000 years ago. There are also 500-year-old cedars. The Rockwood Conservation Area isn't exactly wilderness, but it offers an interesting walk that removes you from our increasingly urban world. There are some great shops and cafés in Rockwood. This is a great hike if you have houseguests.

## Nicola's Insider Info

**LENGTH**
5.1 kilometres

**LEVEL OF DIFFICULTY**
Easy

**LENGTH OF TIME**
1.5 to 2 hour

**NUMBER OF STEPS**
7,599

**kCAL BURNED** 204

**HIGHLIGHTS**
Potholes (unique geology), Eramosa River, caves, old cedars, ruins, fabulous lookout!

**PLACES TO EAT/DRINK**
Eramosa River Café (closed Sun.), Heaven on 7 Bistro & Pub (closed Mon./Tues.) in Rockwood

**ENTRANCE FEE**
Adult $6.64/Senior (65+) $5.31/Child (6–14) $2.65/ Child (<6) free)

**TRAILHEAD**
N43° 36.693' W80° 08.902'

GPS

TRAIL MARKER
*Loop 30*

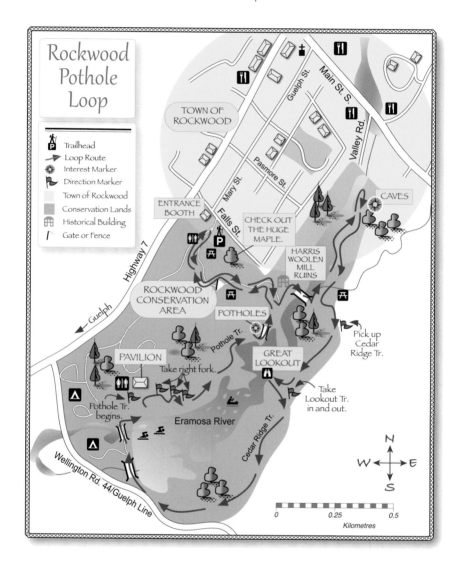

# Rockwood Pothole Loop

**Legend:**
- **P** Trailhead
- Loop Route
- Interest Marker
- Direction Marker
- Town of Rockwood
- Conservation Lands
- Historical Building
- Gate or Fence

TOWN OF ROCKWOOD

Guelph St.
Main St. S.
Valley Rd.
Pasmore St.
Mary St.
Falls St.
Highway 7
Guelph

CAVES

ENTRANCE BOOTH

CHECK OUT THE HUGE MAPLE.

HARRIS WOOLEN MILL RUINS

ROCKWOOD CONSERVATION AREA

POTHOLES

Pick up Cedar Ridge Tr.

Pothole Tr.

GREAT LOOKOUT

PAVILION

Take right fork.

Take Lookout Tr. in and out.

Pothole Tr. begins.

Eramosa River

Cedar Ridge Tr.

Wellington Rd. 44/Guelph Line

N
W — E
S

0        0.25        0.5

Kilometres

*"I hike for the physical challenge, the meditative aspects and the pure joy of being in wild places."*

LINDY MECHEFSKE

# Directions

1.  Park in the Rockwood Conservation Area in the lot to the left of the entrance booth.

2.  From the parking area, look for a grey brick building that has washrooms and a sign that says "Staff Only." Facing this building, turn left and follow the paved road that separates the parking lot from the building.

3.  You come to a set of metal gates that are normally closed. Pass by them and head downhill on the paved road. When you come to a fork in the road, veer right, which takes you toward the ruins.

4.  The ruins of the Harris Woolen Mill sit next to the Eramosa River. You can read the information signs. Built by John Harris in 1884, this limestone structure replaced the original mill he built in 1867. The mill closed in 1925 when it couldn't compete with larger competitors in Toronto and Cambridge.

5.  Walk past the mill, between it and the river, and continue until you come to a bridge. Cross the bridge, noting the remains of a dam to your left.

6.  Walk toward 2 metal signs, turn left and then proceed straight ahead along a small road with the river on your left.

7.  You come to some caves in a cliff on your right. A few are at ground level, and I wandered inside. It was cool and dark, and there was water dripping from the ceiling. Kinda creepy unless you are into spelunking, as cave-exploring is known.

*Ruins of the Harris Woolen Mill.*

*Southern Ontario at its best.*

8. After visiting the caves, return along the same road.

9. When you come to the trail information signs near the bridge, turn left and follow the Cedar Ridge Tr. up the hill on a wide path.

10. The trail passes through a scraggy forest with lots of cedar trees. Eastern white cedars (*Thuja occidentalis*) are a type of cypress that grows in wet areas and in places, such as cliffs, where there is little competition from other trees. Later in this hike, signs describe cliff-dwelling cedars that are up to 500 years old. Parts of the cedar tree contain vitamin C and were used by the Iroquois to prevent and treat scurvy. The person who tested this route for me also noted that there were some alternate-leaf (pagoda) dogwoods.

11. When you come to a small signpost for the Lookout Tr., turn right, following this short, poorly marked, in-and-out path. The view from the lookout is a highlight of the hike. It offers a spectacular look at the Eramosa River below.

12. Return to the Cedar Ridge Tr. via the same route, turn right and continue on your way.

13. The trail drops down and the Cedar Ridge Tr. ends as you pass over a nice old concrete bridge and then a newer one. The Eramosa rushes over a dam to leave the lake under the 2nd bridge.

14. Ahead is a large sandy beach where people can picnic. Although there was still a bit of snow on the ground the day I was there, a few kids were wading in the water!

15. After crossing the 2nd bridge, leave the road and veer right toward the beach. Before you come to the swimming area, turn left, heading away from the water and toward the Pavilion.

16. Just before the steps to the Pavilion, a trail heads off to your right. There is a sign that says "Pothole Tr." It tells you about some of the geology.

17. Pass the sign, heading into the forest. Soon, a trail branches to your left, but stay right. Small interpretive signs along this trail are helpful.

18. At the next fork in the trail, turn right toward "Mill Ruins."

19. Look for potholes along this stretch. Most of them are not completely round holes. Instead, keep an eye out for the rounded sides of partial holes. They are quite easy to spot after you see your first one.

20. Cross over a longish bridge. At the far end, look for a pothole to your right. It was the best one I saw.

21. Way too soon, the trail comes to a road. Turn left here and follow the road back up hill to the parking lot and your car.

*A great way to spend a day.*

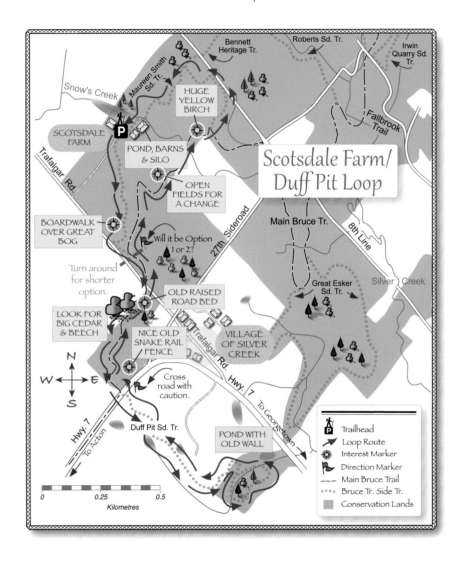

Scotsdale Farm/ Duff Pit Loop

"To hike or not to hike? That is the question."

ROBIN BARFOOT

# Scotsdale Farm/Duff Pit Loop (Georgetown/Glen Williams)

## OVERVIEW

This loop starts and ends at Scotsdale Farm. Donated by the Bennett Family in 1982, it's a magnificent, 215ha piece of property with a stately home and a barn "complex." The Friends of Scotsdale Farm (**www.scotsdalefarm.ca**) are actively involved in its operation and care. I'd love to see it turned back into a working farm. Please take the time to visit their website and possibly encourage them — with words and a donation — to put more life into Scotsdale Farm.

The presence of Scotsdale Farm makes this a distinct hiking experience because the trail crosses agricultural land. I love to see fields, especially when there is a crop growing or one that has just been harvested. As well as farm fields, this loop has wetlands, forests, incredible old-growth trees, an old pond and reservoir, and a waterfall. The barns and silo are fabulous.

One of the six women who tested this route is married to one of my high school English teachers. When he saw the hike directions, he pulled out his red pen "for old times' sake." I just want him to know that he was reading a draft, unedited version of the directions!

*If you want to enjoy hiking in Halton from your doorstep, contact Jill Johnson at Royal LePage Meadowtowne Realty (905-873-5592). Read about her hiking for charity activities at* **www.jilljohnson.ca.**

### Nicola's
## Insider Info

**LENGTH**
11.2 kilometres
(4.2k option)

**LEVEL OF DIFFICULTY**
Easy

**LENGTH OF TIME**
2.5 to 3.75 hours
(1 to 1.5 hours)

**NUMBER OF STEPS**
15,455

**kCAL BURNED** 650

**HIGHLIGHTS**
Old birch, cedar, maple and oak trees; pond; reservoir; falls; Scotsdale Farm; boardwalk through wetlands

**PLACES TO EAT/DRINK**
Heather's Bakery, Silvercreek Socialhaus, The St. George Pub, Symposium Café Restaurant & Lounge in Georgetown/ Kit's Little Kitchen, The Glen Tavern, Copper Kettle Pub in Glen Williams/Glen Williams also has the Williams Mill Art Centre and antique stores

**ENTRANCE FEE** n/a

**TRAILHEAD**
N43° 41.245′W79° 59.443′

**BRUCE TRAIL MAP** 13

GPS

**TRAIL MARKER**
Loop 31

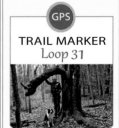

# Directions

1. Park in one of two designated parking lots at Scotsdale Farm. The entrance is from Trafalgar Rd., north of Georgetown.

2. Walk from the parking lot toward the driveway, with the main house on your left.

3. Turn right onto the driveway, walking toward Trafalgar Rd. This is the Bennett Heritage Tr., which has the blue blazes of a Bruce Tr. side trail.

4. A short 300m up the driveway, the trail turns left and enters the forest. Follow it and its blue blazes.

5. The Bennett Heritage Tr. ends as you near Trafalgar Rd. This is where you have to decide if you want to hike the entire 11.2k or the shorter, 4.2k option.

## Longer Option *(11.2k total hike)*

6. Pick up the white blazes of the main Bruce Tr. The main trail goes both to the right and to the left. Go right, continuing on a trail and lengthy boardwalk through a swamp, which parallels Trafalgar Rd.

7. Cross Trafalgar Rd. with caution.

8. On the far side of Trafalgar Rd., the trail continues. For the next few hundred metres, walk along a really lovely trail that must have been an old quarry road or maybe a railway, as it is raised above the wet forest floor. We noticed an uncharacteristically tall Eastern white cedar just off the trail to the left. It had odd pompom-like foliage on top (N43° 40.543′W79° 59.405′). It's tricky to see, especially in summer.

*Snake rail cedar fence.*

9. Just before you come to another road crossing, notice an old snake rail fence. These fences were favoured because they are self-supporting and therefore don't require postholes. On the downside, they take a lot of split rails. Cedar is the preferred material for the rails because it's naturally more resistant to rot than most types of wood.

10. Carefully cross the road (Hwy. 7), turn left and continue walking. Look for a miniature boardwalk crossing the roadside ditch and blue blazes. You leave the main Bruce Tr. here and follow the Duff Pit Side Tr.

11. I'd never walked this trail before and wasn't sure it would be worth a 2.4k diversion along an in-and-out trail. As it turns out, it leads into a beautiful mature forest. You pass by a small pond that is held back by a dam and bordered on one side by a laid stone wall. There is a pipe in the middle and, according to the Bruce Tr. guide, it was a reservoir.

*Raised trail through cedar forest.*

12. Further along, there is a waterfall that may be obscured in summer. This stream is the western branch of Silver Creek.

13. The Duff Pit Side Tr. forms a loop through the forest and then follows the same route back to the road.

14. When you return to Hwy. 7, cross it again with caution. Turn left on the other side and re-enter the forest when you see the white blazes of the main Bruce Tr. (DO NOT go straight ahead along the road.)

15. Follow the main Bruce Tr., retracing your footsteps back over Trafalgar Rd. and over the long and slippery boardwalk.

16. When you come to the junction with the Bennett Heritage Tr., veer right to continue following the white blazes of the main Bruce Tr.

17. I stopped for lunch on a well-placed log here. It was a great spot, protected from the wind on a blustery day in mid-November. It might be buggy in summer.

18. Follow a boardwalk before coming to the 1st of several fields that you skirt. It's nice to get out of the forest and into the open. The trail goes into and out of the forest for the remainder of the route.

19. When you come to a junction where the blue blazes of the Maureen Smith Side Tr. lead straight ahead, take this side trail, leaving the main Bruce Tr. You parallel an old dirt road for a while and then enter a mature woodlot.

*Scotsdale Farm.* PHOTO BY ANNE CROWE

20. Look for an intersection with the Bennett Heritage Tr. and take it. You turn left, leaving the Maureen Smith Side Tr.

21. You come out onto a back entrance to Scotsdale Farm, where there are some great interpretive signs. When I walked along here years ago, it was all fenced off with rolls of barbed wire. Huge signs said something like "No Trespassing: Order of the Government of the United States." It turned out that it was the set for a movie starring Tom Cruise. Perhaps someone knows the name of the movie and can remind me.

22. Follow this old driveway to the farm. There are not a lot of blue blazes, but if you stay on the driveway, you won't get lost.

23. There is a big, stream-fed pond on your right, which I've known to be home to swans. The stream is Snow's Creek, which flows into Silver Creek, which flows into the Credit River just above Glen Williams. The enormous barn complex appears on your left. It's well cared for, but it's sad to see it sitting idle. Barns need to be used — literally. If there are no animals in a barn to minimize the amount of frost that gets into the foundation, it will begin to crumble.

24. Look up to the peak of the old barn and note the series of holes where pigeons might perch. Around the front of the old barn, windows look into now-empty box stalls for horses.

25. Keep going, and around the next corner there is a beautiful old silo. Grain is stored in these cylindrical structures.

26. Keep following the driveway until you return to your car.

## Shorter Option (4.2k total hike)

1. Continued from Point #5 on page 172.

2. Pick up the white blazes of the main Bruce Tr. The main trail goes both to the right and to the left. You go left, heading into the forest.

3. Go to Point #17 on page 173.

# Sixteen Mile Creek Loop
## (Oakville)

## OVERVIEW

I set off on this loop, which is courtesy of the Pathfinders Hiking Group of Oakville (**www. oakvillepathfinders.blogspot.ca**), on a hot, muggy day. When we drove into a subdivision in Oakville, my 2 hiking pals were skeptical. They'd both expected a wander through the rural countryside. Metres later, we were in the trees, and though we could look into people's backyards for the first half kilometre, we caught tantalizing glimpses of the green Sixteen Mile Creek valley below us. Once we dropped down to what is more river than creek by southern Ontario standards, we forgot that we were in the city. The birds and the running water drowned out any city sounds, and we hoped the fish were biting for the fisherman. You are down in the valley for about half of this hike. We saw a Baltimore oriole, the cutest adolescent robins that hadn't completely shed their baby feathers and a somewhat rare milk snake.

This hike is not quite rural, but it's not urban either. If you don't live in Oakville, it's still worth it to see Sixteen Mile Creek and then to visit downtown Oakville for a latte, of course.

**32**

## Nicola's
## Insider Info

**LENGTH**
7 kilometres

**LEVEL OF DIFFICULTY**
Moderate

**LENGTH OF TIME**
1.5 to 2.5 hours

**NUMBER OF STEPS**
8,607

**kCAL BURNED** 295

**HIGHLIGHTS**
Sixteen Mile Creek valley, urban/rural combo, views, peace in the city

**PLACES TO EAT/DRINK**
Tribeca Coffee Co. is a great supporter of my hiking guides and has great coffee! Vereda Central Coffee Roasters, Monastery Bakery, Aroma Espresso Bar, Bean There, Kerr Street Café, Stoney's Bread Co., Taste of Colombia in Oakville

**ENTRANCE FEE** n/a

**TRAILHEAD**
N43° 27.134′W79° 44.104′

**GPS**

TRAIL MARKER
Loop 32

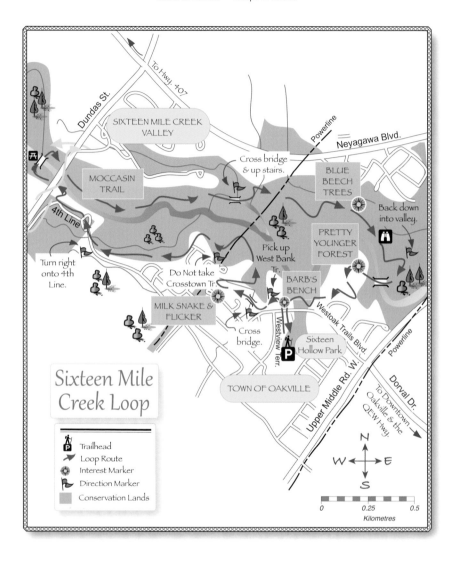

**Sixteen Mile Creek Loop**

To Hwy. 407

Dundas St.

SIXTEEN MILE CREEK VALLEY

MOCCASIN TRAIL

4th Line

Turn right onto 4th Line.

Cross bridge & up stairs.

Powerline

Neyagawa Blvd.

BLUE BEECH TREES

Back down into valley.

PRETTY YOUNGER FOREST

Pick up West Bank Tr.

Do Not take Crosstown Tr.

BARB'S BENCH

Westoak Trails Blvd.

Powerline

MILK SNAKE & FLICKER

Cross bridge.

Westview Terr.

Sixteen Hollow Park

TOWN OF OAKVILLE

Upper Middle Rd. W.

To Downtown Oakville & the QEW Hwy.

Dorval Dr.

**Legend**

P Trailhead
Loop Route
Interest Marker
Direction Marker
Conservation Lands

N
W — E
S

0    0.25    0.5
Kilometres

*"We hiked near Belfountain last weekend. We ate our own lunch on the trail and finished off with an ice cream in town. We live in Toronto in an area with lots of trees, but we feel disconnected from true nature."*

TED PARKINSON & PAT DALES

# Directions

1. There is parking in a small lot in Sixteen Hollow Park, which is just north of the intersection of Upper Middle Rd. W and Dorval Dr. in Oakville.

2. Leave the parking lot heading back toward Westoak Trails Blvd., the street you entered the parking lot from.

3. Cross Westoak Trails Blvd. and look for a sign for the West Bank Tr. as well as a bench that has a plaque dedicated to Barbara Laird. The ravine will be on your right.

4. Turn left and follow the town-maintained trail along a wide cinder path and across a bridge.

5. At the trail intersection, continue following the West Bank Tr.

6. You catch glimpses of the very deep Sixteen Mile Creek valley along here. We also saw a Northern flicker, with its nice white bum. We scared up this woodpecker from the ground, which is normal since they dig for bugs and worms.

7. The trail takes you around a half loop. Stay on the most obvious path, ignoring smaller ones that veer off every now and again.

8. I almost stepped on a milk snake (*Lampropeltis triangulum*) along here. This non-venomous snake is listed as a species of Special Concern in Ontario because its numbers are dwindling, mostly due to habitat loss. It's often mistaken for a Massasauga rattlesnake because it rattles leaves with its tail to make a noise that can be mistaken for that made by its venomous cousin.

9. When you finish this half loop, continue following the West Bank Tr. DO NOT take the Crosstown Tr. You pass by a cemetery and a few homes. Drop down and then turn right onto 4th Line.

10. Follow this derelict road down and then up again. At the end of 4th Line, cross the turnaround, go through the yellow barriers and follow the West Bank Tr. down a steep hill. (If the steep hill is closed, take the 4th Line to Dundas St. Head north, cross the bridge and turn right onto Lion's Valley Park Rd. and follow it to the parking lot in #12 below.

*I almost stepped on this milk snake.*

11. You are now in the Sixteen Mile Creek valley. Walk under the high overpass for Dundas St. toward the bridge over the creek. There is a nice picnic area here.

*This is an immature robin that hasn't yet lost its fuzz.*

12. Cross the bridge, turn right, cross the parking lot and pick up the trail as it passes by a pillar for the overpass. This stretch of lovely trail was recently renamed the Moccasin Tr. to acknowledge that Oakville sits on ancestral land of the Mississaugas of the Credit First Nation.

13. Cross a little bridge and head up the stairs. At the top, take the obvious trail to the right that skirts the top of the valley.

14. At the T-intersection of trails, turn right, following the Inner Valley Tr. There are a couple of great lookouts. We came across a blue beech tree (*Carpinus caroliniana*). They are also known as musclewood trees because the smooth ridges on their trunks make them look like muscles.

15. Follow the trail as it heads down into the valley again. At the bottom, turn right and cross the bridge over Sixteen Mile Creek. This is where we saw a Baltimore oriole. The forest through here is lovely, with tall adolescent hardwood trees interspersed by a few big grandma and grandpa maples.

*Blue beech or musclewood tree.*

16. At the next T-intersection of trails, go left and uphill. At the top of the incline, go right, following the West Bank Tr.

17. At the Y-intersection, go right and you are back at Barb's bench and your car.

# Speyside North Route
(Milton/Speyside)

## OVERVIEW

In the original version of *Halton Hikes*, I included a loop that went south from Speyside, but with the closure of a Bruce Trail side trail, that loop was no longer possible. So I had to go back to the drawing board. Where the Bruce Trail taketh away, however, the Bruce Trail giveth back! A good loop heading north was there before me and I decided to check it out.

Like its predecessor, this Speyside route is rocky and swampy. Don't tell anyone I said this, but after a while I find that walking on a rocky trail gets a bit tiresome. Fortunately, the rocks gave way before I came to that point. Also fortunately, I love swamps more than I dislike rocky trails, and this loop has enough swamps to keep a swamp lover like me happy as a pig in you know what.

I also enjoyed the sumac tunnel and discovered several welcoming creek-side stops. There were even open fields that gave me some relief from the forest shade. In the end, I think I like this Speyside North route better than the Speyside South loop it replaced. I hope you enjoy it, too.

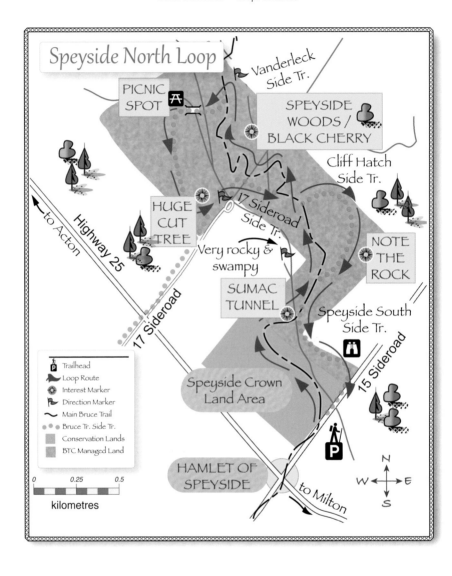

Speyside North Loop

*"Whenever I hike, I feel a connection with the original inhabitants of the land. This is how they travelled — quietly, on foot, alive to the wilderness surrounding them."*

DON FERGUSON

# Directions

1. Park on 15 Sideroad, about 300m east of Hwy. 25. It's about 8k south of Acton in the hamlet of Speyside. There's space on both sides of 15 Sideroad for a total of about 10 cars.

2. In 2019, a friend and I spent 2 weeks hiking in Scotland along the Speyside Way Whisky Trail. En route, we passed (and visited!) many of Scotland's renowned distilleries, including Glenfiddich and Glenlivet, among dozens of others. (We didn't visit them all.) It was a fabulous trip. Sadly, Ontario's Speyside is not much more than a busy crossroad. Scottish people would be surprised.

*This lonely rock is surely a landmark on this trail.*

3. On the north side of 15 Sideroad, look for two stones with a path between them. They're to the right of a Bruce Tr. sign attached to a tree.

4. For virtually this entire loop, you follow either the blue or white blazes of the Bruce Tr. So, if you find yourself walking on a path without these blazes (there are several), turn back; you have missed a turn.

5. Follow the trail between the rocks into the Speyside Crown Land Area, owned by the Ministry of Natural Resources and Forestry, following the main Bruce Tr.'s white blazes.

6. Almost immediately bypass the blue-blazed Speyside South Side Tr. About 10 minutes later, you come to a great sumac tunnel. It was tunnel-like in April without foliage or sumac's characteristic red berries. Sumac is a member of the poison ivy family (some relatives!). Invasive, but cheerful, bright-yellow coltsfoot was in bloom, along with bloodroot and sharp-lobed hepatica in pink, white and mauve.

7. Pass by the Speyside South Side Tr. (other end) and the Cliff Hatch Side Tr., staying with the main Bruce Tr.'s white blazes.

8. The trail becomes very rocky and tricky as it passes through numerous "swamps," which were alive with guttural, probably leopard, frogs.

9. Look for a sharp, righthand turn and bypass the 17 Sideroad Side Tr.

*A sumac tunnel.*

Continue along the main Bruce Tr. for another 1k (20 minutes). Note a large eastern hemlock (with sign) and later, a display sign about Speyside Woods. When you arrive at the blue-blazed Vanderleck Side Tr., turn left leaving the main Bruce Tr. (Ignore the sign about the 13.4k loop.)

10. Up ahead is a great picnic spot by a small stream. The trail then passes through a beautiful maple forest where there's a spectacular double-trunked black cherry tree with cornflake-like bark. The Vanderleck Side Tr. ends at 17 Sideroad.

11. Turn left onto 17 Sideroad, following it to its end, where you pick up the blue-blazed 17 Sideroad Side Tr. as it enters the forest on the left side of the road. Note the huge tree trunk that has been left here.

12. Cross 3 small bridges through beautiful swamps until you arrive back at the main Bruce Tr. Turn right onto the white-blazed main Bruce Tr.

13. Turn left onto the blue-blazed Cliff Hatch Side Tr. Along the way, bypass a large rock that blocks an old trail.

14. At the main Bruce Tr., turn left, following its white blazes past remnants of a stone wall and back into the sumac tunnel.

15. Mid-tunnel, veer left onto the Speyside South Side Tr., entering an open field that leads you into a forest where there's a view of open farmland with Mississauga's skyscrapers in the distance.

16. The trail leads you back onto 15 Sideroad, where you turn right to find your car.

*I love swamps.*

# Terra Cotta
# Footpath Loop (Terra Cotta)

*You require a day pass to enter the Terra Cotta Conservation Area. To get yours online, visit https://store.cvc.ca.*

## OVERVIEW

It wasn't possible to walk this exact route when I wrote the first edition of *Halton Hikes: Loops & Lattes*. But five years later, there it was. And what a wonderful route it is. Almost free of walking on roads, it's a great option for people with dogs and those who need some relief from civilization.

It's next door to the village of Terra Cotta, which was once known as Salmonville because these fish were so prolific in the Credit River. Its other claim to fame is the red clay, some of which appears on this hike. It gave rise to the village's current name.

There are some magnificent old trees near the beginning and along other parts of this loop. Later on, you might spy some shagbark hickories. There are streams, meadows and ponds. It covers a lot of ground, and you end up not far from the Terra Cotta Inn, where you can stop for a white-linen dinner upstairs or a brew and burger downstairs in the pub.

So hit this loop and have a good time of it.

> *"When I take the first couple of steps into a forest, I take a deep breath and sigh; it's therapy for the soul and makes me smile."*
>
> NIKOLA BOADWAY

### Nicola's
# Insider Info

**LENGTH**
12 kilometres

**LEVEL OF DIFFICULTY**
Moderate

**LENGTH OF TIME**
3 to 4 hours

**NUMBER OF STEPS**
16,776

**kCAL BURNED** 690

**HIGHLIGHTS**
Long, nearly roadless loop, gorgeous old-growth trees, ponds and rocky path

**PLACES TO EAT/DRINK**
The Glen Tavern, Copper Kettle Pub, Kit's Little Kitchen in Glen Williams, Terra Cotta Inn & Pub, Terra Cotta Country Store in Terra Cotta

**ENTRANCE FEE**
Adult $5.75/Senior (60+) $4.43/Child (6–14) $2.65/Child (<6) free Weekend and holiday parking can be reserved for $10

**TRAILHEAD**
N43° 43.617′ W79° 57.530′

**BRUCE TRAIL MAP** 14

TRAIL MARKER
Loop 34

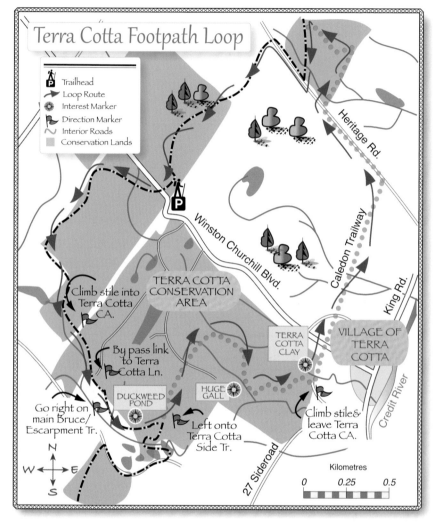

# Terra Cotta Footpath Loop

**Legend:**
- Trailhead
- Loop Route
- Interest Marker
- Direction Marker
- Interior Roads
- Conservation Lands

Heritage Rd.

Caledon Trailway

King Rd.

Winston Churchill Blvd.

Climb stile into Terra Cotta CA.

TERRA COTTA CONSERVATION AREA

By pass link to Terra Cotta Ln.

TERRA COTTA CLAY

VILLAGE OF TERRA COTTA

Credit River

Go right on main Bruce/ Escarpment Tr.

DUCKWEED POND

HUGE GALL

Climb stile & leave Terra Cotta CA.

Left onto Terra Cotta Side Tr.

27 Sideroad

N
W — E
S

Kilometres

0    0.25    0.5

# Directions

1. Park at the top of the hill about 500m north of the entrance to the Terra Cotta Conservation Area on Winston Churchill Blvd. There is roadside parking on the east side of the road.

2. Walk north along the Winston Churchill Blvd. to the sign-posted trail access points and turn left (west) onto the main Bruce Tr.

3. The rocky trail passes by vernal ponds where a diverse collection of wildflowers decorates the trail.

*This is duckweed. It is natural and healthy.* PHOTO BY LINDA PIM

4. There are some enormous sugar maples and other hardwoods along this section of trail. Also listen for the "teacher, teacher, teacher" call of ovenbirds.

5. Cross a bridge and a small wetland, and look for common buckthorn, which is considered an invasive species. The small trees spread vigorously, aided by birds who eat, but cannot digest, the seeds.

6. The trail runs along the top of a ridge. Listen here for Rogers Cr., a tributary to the Credit River. It's below and to your right.

7. Climb a stile and enter the Terra Cotta Conservation Area. Trails within the conservation area are marked with trail names, as well as Bruce Tr. blazes.

8. At a Y-intersection, follow the yellow Vaughan Tr. to the right, which is also marked with the Bruce Tr.'s white blazes. You will be following the Bruce Tr.'s white or blue blazes for almost this entire loop.

9. Bypass the Trail Link to Terra Cotta Lane, following the main Bruce Tr./ Vaughn Tr. (yellow) downhill into one of the prettiest sections of forest on this route.

10. At the next intersection, turn right onto the joint main Bruce Tr./ Escarpment Tr. (red).

11. The trail descends more steeply. As it levels out, there's a cattail-lined pond on the left. By mid-June, the pond is covered with duckweed, a common aquatic plant. This is a natural and healthy process. Amy, who helped with this route, came across someone hiking here with their cat on a leash.

12. At the T-intersection with the Graydon Tr. (green), turn left onto the blue-blazed Terra Cotta Side Tr.

13. The path curves sharply to the left, crosses a wide boardwalk and arrives at a trail intersection. Turn right here to continue following Terra Cotta Side Tr./ the Graydon Tr. (green).

14. At the intersection with Forest Meadow Lane, continue straight on the Terra Cotta Side Tr./Graydon Tr. (green).

15. Look for some beautiful oak trees along this narrow section of trail that descends into an area carpeted with jewel weed.

16. Cross a bridge and, as you climb, look for an oak tree with an enormous gall. Wood turners love making bowls out of galls. They are the result of insect damage.

*You enter the Terra Cotta Conservation Area here.*

17. At a T-intersection with the A.F. Coventry Tr., turn right continuing to follow the Terra Cotta Side Tr./Graydon Tr.

18. Continue straight past the next intersection with the A.F. Coventry Tr. until you come to a stile marking the end of the conservation area. After climbing the stile, turn around and look to your right to see a small slope of the red clay soil that gives Terra Cotta its name. Turn left at Mile Zero of the Caledon Trailway, which is marked with the Terra Cotta Side Tr.'s blue blazes.

19. Carefully cross Winston Churchill Blvd. and Isabella St. When you come to Heritage Rd., turn left still following the blue blazes.

20. Follow the Terra Cotta Side Tr. when it turns right and leaves the road.

21. The Terra Cotta Side Tr. ends at an intersection with the main Bruce Tr. Turn left here onto the main Bruce Tr. Follow it until it returns to Heritage Rd.

22. Cross Heritage Rd. and turn right continuing to follow the main Bruce Tr.'s white blazes.

23. After 400m, the trail turns left and re-enters the forest, crosses a small boardwalk and then climbs up the escarpment through a rocky landscape. Enjoy the view at the top, foliage-allowing.

24. The trail passes through mixed hardwoods, then some pine plantations. Keep following the white blazes past remnants of a stone wall that indicates this was once farmland.

25. When you arrive at Winston Churchill Blvd., turn left and head back to your car.

# Terra Cotta
# Wolf Lake Loop

## OVERVIEW

This loop packs a lot into 5k. It starts out rolling up and down a root-infested trail and past towering oak trees. Keep an eye out for shagbark hickories. I've included a photo of their shaggy bark to help you identify them. Soon the trail turns into a wide lane, which is perfect for walking 2 or 3 abreast and having a good gab.

Wolf Lake was covered in water lilies as I walked by it, which was a completely different scene from when I skated on it last February. This time out, I spied a tunnel-like path that ran through rushes and into the water — an indication that beavers were around. Next up is Muskrat Pond, followed by a wander through a wetland that has been reclaimed from what was a clay-lined "pool" when I was a kid. We used to beg our mum to take us to the Terra Cotta Conservation Area because the water was warm and because there was a concession stand where we purchased candy necklaces and Sweetarts. Once called Salmonville, Terra Cotta was the place to catch Atlantic salmon until the late 1800s.

*Want to hike two days in a row? Spend a peaceful night at the **Peartree B&B** in Terra Cotta. It's worth it for the breakfast alone. (**www.peartreebnb.com**)*

## Nicola's
## Insider Info

**LENGTH**
5 kilometres

**LEVEL OF DIFFICULTY**
Easy

**LENGTH OF TIME**
1 to 1.5 hours

**NUMBER OF STEPS**
6,433

**kCAL BURNED** 255

**HIGHLIGHTS**
Wolf Lake, oak trees, shagbark hickory, wide open lane

**PLACES TO EAT/DRINK**
Terra Cotta Inn & Pub,
Terra Cotta Country Store
(open summer weekends)

**ENTRANCE FEE**
Adult $5.75/Senior (60+)
$4.43/Child (6–14)
$2.65/Child (<6) free

**TRAILHEAD**
N43° 43.393'W79° 57.435'

**BRUCE TRAIL MAP** 14

**GPS**
**TRAIL MARKER**
*Loop 35*

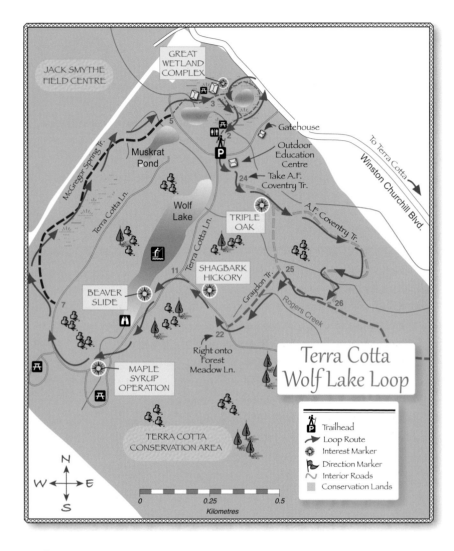

Terra Cotta
Wolf Lake Loop

## Directions

1. Enter the Terra Cotta Conservation Area from Winston Churchill Blvd. Park in Lot 1, if possible.

2. From the large information kiosk, look directly behind you to the far side of the parking lot for a cinder path with a small grey sign that points toward the Outdoor Education Centre. Follow it across a road and through yellow barriers. At Station 12, turn left taking the Trail Link (not Terra Cotta Lane).

Follow signs for the A.F. Coventry Tr. past the Outdoor Education Centre, which is on your left.

3. At Station 24, turn right onto the A.F. Coventry Tr., taking the left path where it splits in two. Alan F. Coventry was a professor and advisory member of Credit Valley Conservation.

4. After a little over 1k walking through a mature forest and over several bridges, you arrive at Station 26. Turn right here onto the Graydon Tr.

5. At Station 25, turn left, still following the Graydon Tr. and cross another bridge. Notice the red clay stream bed that gives Terra Cotta its name. There are several shagbark hickories to your right along here. Native to Ontario, it's slow-growing and can be tall.

6. At Station 22, go right onto Forest Meadow Lane.

7. At Station 11, turn left onto Terra Cotta Lane. You're beginning your walk around Wolf Lake.

8. Look for tunnel-like trails through the rushes to your left, which would have been built by beavers. These amazing rodents are Canada's national emblem. According to David Suzuki, beavers are "perhaps the most important animal on the planet." The series of ponds and wetlands you are about to explore wouldn't be the same without these water engineers.

9. Stay on Terra Cotta Lane as it goes around the lake and offers some good lookouts. Fishing is allowed in these ponds.

10. As you round the lake, you see blue tubing that connects some trees. This is the modern way of collecting sap from maple trees for conversion into our famed maple syrup.

11. On the far side of Wolf Lake, turn left at Station 7 onto McGregor Spring Tr. It's a pretty walk through the forest, past a small wetland and over a couple of springs, one of which must be McGregor Spring.

*Shagbark hickory.*

*Muskrat Pond.*

12. You come to a rail fence with Muskrat Pond to your right. At the end of this pond, things get a bit tricky, so follow these directions carefully.

13. At Station 5, the McGregor Spring Tr. ends. Pass the Station 5 and cross the paved road, following Trail Link signs to P3.

14. When you come to a building, turn right and walk past it so it's to your left. Then walk diagonally across a parking lot in front of an open-air pavilion, which will be on your left.

15. Leave the parking lot, looking for Station 3, which is the start of the Wetland Tr. There are interesting interpretive signs.

16. When I was young, this area was a popular swimming spot. The photo taken in the 1950s (before I was there!) is pretty much what I remember. We loved swimming here because the water was warm and there was a concession stand!

17. Turn right onto the boardwalk that crosses the wetland. You will be walking a figure 8.

18. At the end of the boardwalk, turn left, walk around the wetland until you arrive back at the boardwalk. Turn left here and cross the boardwalk a second time. Turn right at the end of the boardwalk. Walk through a picnic area.

19. At Station 2, follow the sign for P1 (if you parked in P1). Walk to the left of the building with bathrooms and pass through the archway into P1 where your car is parked.

# Walking Fern/
# Silver Creek Loop
(Glen Williams)

## OVERVIEW

Walking ferns may not have the same cachet as spirit bears, but they are rare. And while it will cost you dearly to get to spirit bear territory and there is no guarantee that you'll spy one when you get there, I can assure you that walking ferns abound on this hike. So, lace up your boots and get out on this spectacular, rocky route that begins with a short in-and-out trail that is populated with all kinds of ferns, including the rare walking fern (*Asplenium rhizophyllum*), which you should look at but not touch. It grows on the northern rocky side of the Niagara Escarpment and derives its name from the fact that it forms a new root at the tip of its long slender leaves. In this way it "walks."

This trail passes enormous trees as it winds through a beautiful forest that's strewn with moss-covered rocks. I walked it on a drizzly day with a gusty wind that had the trees swaying as though they were sweeping the heavens clean. I ran into a group of hikers from Elora, and they were also wet, but happy to be out enjoying the trails that make this one of the best routes in this guidebook.

### 36

## Nicola's
## Insider Info

**LENGTH**
8.9 kilometres

**LEVEL OF DIFFICULTY**
Moderate

**LENGTH OF TIME**
2 to 3 hours

**NUMBER OF STEPS**
12,760

**kCAL BURNED** 511

**HIGHLIGHTS**
West Coast-like trail, walking ferns, lookout, fabulous forest, rugged Niagara Escarpment rocks, boardwalk alongside the pond

**PLACES TO EAT/DRINK**
Kit's Little Kitchen, The Glen Tavern, Copper Kettle Pub in Glen Williams/Terra Cotta Inn & Pub, Terra Cotta Country Store (open summer weekends) in Terra Cotta

**ENTRANCE FEE**
Donation box

**TRAILHEAD**
N43° 42.572'W79° 57.775'

**BRUCE TRAIL MAP** 13

GPS
TRAIL MARKER
Loop 36

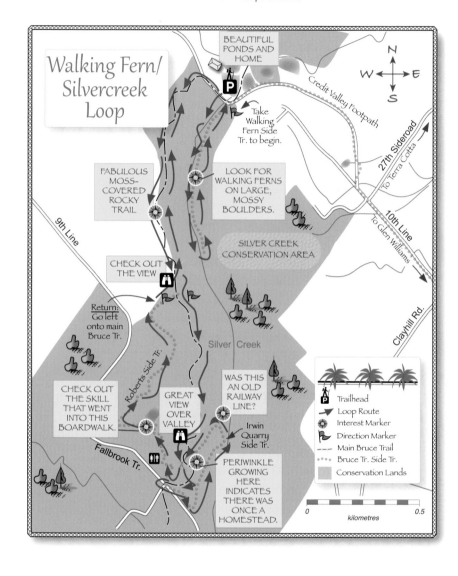

# Walking Fern/ Silvercreek Loop

BEAUTIFUL PONDS AND HOME

Take Walking Fern Side Tr. to begin.

Credit Valley Footpath

27th Sideroad
To Terra Cotta

10th Line
To Glen Williams

FABULOUS MOSS-COVERED ROCKY TRAIL

LOOK FOR WALKING FERNS ON LARGE, MOSSY BOULDERS.

9th Line

SILVER CREEK CONSERVATION AREA

CHECK OUT THE VIEW

Return: Go left onto main Bruce Tr.

Silver Creek

Clayhill Rd.

Roberts Side Tr.

CHECK OUT THE SKILL THAT WENT INTO THIS BOARDWALK.

GREAT VIEW OVER VALLEY

WAS THIS AN OLD RAILWAY LINE?

Irwin Quarry Side Tr.

Fallbrook Tr.

PERIWINKLE GROWING HERE INDICATES THERE WAS ONCE A HOMESTEAD.

Trailhead
Loop Route
Interest Marker
Direction Marker
Main Bruce Trail
Bruce Tr. Side Tr.
Conservation Lands

0       kilometres       0.5

*"Even on the worst weather days or when
I didn't feel up for a hike, once I'm out there,
I'm always glad I chose to do it. "*

AL AXWORTHY

# Directions

*Walking ferns.*

1. Park on the west side of 10th Line in Halton Hills, north of 27th Sideroad, at the bottom of the valley, across the road from a beautiful old house surrounded by lovely ponds. There is plenty of room on the wide shoulder for several cars.

2. Follow the blue blazes of the Walking Fern Side Tr. It's an in-and-out, 850m trail that passes through fern-laden rocky outcrops (1.7k in total). Keep your eyes open for the walking ferns, which grow on moss-covered boulders. I only spied these very un-fern-like ferns on the uphill side of the trail.

3. There is a lovely patch at N43° 42.378′ W79° 57.893′. Look but don't touch.

4. The end of the trail is marked by a vertical blue blaze topped by a horizontal one. You turn around here and return along the same route, keeping your eyes open for more walking ferns.

5. At the road where you parked, turn left and pick up the white blazes of the main Bruce Tr. as it turns immediately left again and leaves the road.

6. The trail is often mucky at the beginning because you are walking on Queenston shale. With its characteristic red colour, this gummy clay accounts for nearby Terra Cotta being so named. It is a clue that you are walking on the Niagara Escarpment.

7. Climb out of the valley, where the red clay gives way to wet mud and rocks, rocks and more rocks. This trail can be an ankle twister, but it's well worth the risk.

8. At the top of your climb, and when the leaves are not out, you can see across the valley through which Silver Creek flows. It's a tributary of the Credit River. On occasion, the trail passes between beautiful moss-covered, rocky outcrops amid dense green cedars, which give the route a rainforest feel. The person who tested this hike for me noted the different colours and textures of tree bark, so take a moment to study the rich collection of tree species in this forest.

*I ran into this group of happy, if wet, hikers from Elora.*

9. Following the main Bruce Tr.'s white blazes, bypass the Roberts Side Tr. and the first of 2 links to the Irwin Quarry Side Tr. Then, just before reaching a dirt road called Fallbrook Tr., look for the second link to the Irwin Quarry Side Tr. There are information signs and washrooms here.

10. Leave the main Bruce Tr., by turning left onto the blue-blazed Irwin Quarry Side Tr. It drops down into and then out of the valley.

11. After about 1k, the ground is covered in lovely but invasive periwinkle that has pretty purple flowers in the spring. This, as well as some big old trees, indicates that this was likely once a homestead because periwinkle is a non-native ornamental that wouldn't normally be found in an Ontario forest.

12. The Irwin Quarry Side Tr. ends at the main Bruce Tr. Turn left onto the main Bruce Tr. and follow its white blazes back toward Fallbrook Tr.

13. Just before Fallbrook Tr., turn right and follow the blue blazes of the Roberts Side Tr.

14. Pass by a pretty pond with a boardwalk that is great for viewing waterfowl. Also note how the boards in the boardwalk are cut to go around corners. Congrats to the carpenter(s). An incredible amount of work has gone into this construction.

15. After 1.5k, the Roberts Side Tr. ends at the main Bruce Tr. Turn left here and follow the white blazes of the main Bruce Tr. back to your car.

# Waterdown/ Offa's Dyke Loop

## OVERVIEW

During a recent visit to the Sierra Norte Mountains of Mexico, in addition to experiencing an amazing week-long, village-to-village hike, I visited the world's fattest tree: the Tule Tree. (I wrote about both in my blog at https://nicolaross.ca/fab-hiking-in-mexico-who-would-have-thought/) Who couldn't write about a tree that is over 14m in diameter and requires 30 people holding hands to reach all the way around it? During my research, I learned that I was a "dendrophiliac," which means one who loves trees. So it was with great excitement that I saw so many shagbark hickories along this route. I also enjoyed the huge 195-year-old red oak and the 128-year-old bitternut hickory. They are signposted as part of the Bruce Trail's Heritage Tree Program.

The walk along Grindstone Creek and the vistas of Burlington and Toronto are a nice change from looking at all those darn maples and hop horn-beams and basswoods, says the dendrophiliac! Moreover, Waterdown has an array of restaurants, including the Copper Kettle Café where they made me a fine iced latte. Much of the route follows the Offa's Dyke Path Friendship Trail. The Offa's Dyke Path is a 285k footpath that follows the border between England and Wales.

> *Specialty Coffee | Mouth-Watering Food | Tasty Sweets & Treats | Atmosphere* **Copper Kettle Café** *in Waterdown* (**www.copperkettlecafe.ca**)

**37**

## Nicola's Insider Info

**LENGTH**
14.6 kilometres
**LEVEL OF DIFFICULTY**
Moderate
**LENGTH OF TIME**
3.5 to 5 hours
**NUMBER OF STEPS**
21,477
**kCAL BURNED** 653
**HIGHLIGHTS**
Smokey Hollow, Grindstone Creek, shagbark hickory, enormous red oaks, vistas of Burlington and Toronto
**PLACES TO EAT/DRINK**
The Copper Kettle Café is known for its apple fritters. Meanwhile, tea at The White House is also recommended. Other options are the Jitterbug Café and The Royal Coachman pub in Waterdown.
**ENTRANCE FEE** n/a
**TRAILHEAD**
N43° 19.854' W79° 53.220'
**BRUCE TRAIL MAP** 9

**TRAIL MARKER**
*Loop 37*

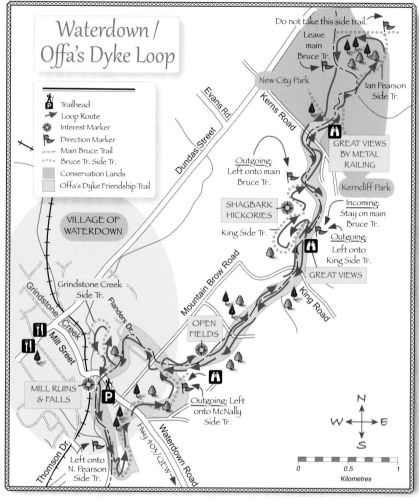

**Waterdown / Offa's Dyke Loop**

Legend:
- Trailhead
- Loop Route
- Interest Marker
- Direction Marker
- --- Main Bruce Trail
- •••• Bruce Tr. Side Tr.
- Conservation Lands
- Offa's Dyke Friendship Trail

VILLAGE OF WATERDOWN

Do not take this side trail.

Leave main Bruce Tr.

New City Park

Ian Pearson Side Tr.

GREAT VIEWS BY METAL RAILING

Kerncliff Park

Outgoing: Left onto main Bruce Tr.

SHAGBARK HICKORIES

King Side Tr.

Incoming: Stay on main Bruce Tr.

Outgoing: Left onto King Side Tr.

GREAT VIEWS

Grindstone Creek Side Tr.

OPEN FIELDS

MILL RUINS & FALLS

Outgoing: Left onto McNally Side Tr.

Left onto N. Pearson Side Tr.

Evans Rd.
Kerns Road
Dundas Street
Mountain Brow Road
King Road
Grindstone Creek
Mill Street
Flanders Dr.
Hwy 403/QEW
Waterdown Road
Thomson Dr.

N W E S

0    0.5    1
Kilometres

## Directions

1. Park in the Smokey Hollow parking lot on the west (right) side of Waterdown Rd./Mill St., just as you enter the village from the south. It's a bit tricky to find.

2. There is a viewing platform overlooking Grindstone Creek and what's left of one of the many mills that once made Waterdown a booming industrial town. As the interpretive sign explains, the mills gave way first to steam power, then electricity and finally to the arrival of a train. But that was long after the area became known as Smokey Hollow because the smoke produced by the mills hung overhead.

3. The hike begins at the signpost that is to your left as you face the creek. Head along the main Bruce Tr. with its white blazes as it parallels the creek, which is on your right. (DO NOT go up the hill and across the road.)

*The world's fattest tree: the Tule Tree in Mexico.*

4. The trail drops down into the river valley and follows alongside pretty Grindstone Creek for about 800m.

5. Keep your eyes open for a trail junction, where you turn left and follow the Norman Pearson Side Tr. with its blue blazes. Dr. Pearson was one of the founding members of the Bruce Tr.

6. The trail climbs up out of the valley and comes out onto a precious little road. I spied an old drive shed near an older cottage and dreamed about turning it into the perfect little house.

7. Still following blue blazes, cross busy Waterdown Rd. with care and continue uphill. Look for the old orchard on your left. The trail enters a forest and meets the McNally Side Tr. The Norman Pearson Side Tr. continues on for another 155m to a lookout. The view was blocked by leaves when I was there but would be great in spring and winter.

8. After visiting the lookout, return to the junction and turn right onto the McNally Side Tr. Follow it to the main Bruce Tr., across land kindly donated by Patrick McNally. He died on June 3, (my birthday!) 2016, at the age of 101, 10 years after donating this $1.2-million property to the Bruce Trail Conservancy — the organization's largest donation at the time.

*These are ice pans. They form near waterfalls.*

PHOTO BY MARY TAYLOR

9. Turn right onto the main Bruce Trail with its white blazes. As I was climbing the stile here, I glimpsed a flash of red. A scarlet tanager, I wondered?

Then there were 2 more flashes. It turned out to be 3 male cardinals flying in the open, which is unusual. I can only guess that they were immature birds following their dad.

10. Climb over a 2nd stile, and then note the shagbark hickories that start to appear in abundance. They seemed to be everywhere, along with tall oaks and many maples.

11. Cross King Rd. and enjoy the vistas to your right. As you make your way along the top of the ridge, the views get better. The Burlington Skyway and Toronto's CN Tower were visible when I walked here.

12. About 500m after crossing the road, you come to the King Side Tr. Leave the main Bruce Tr. and turn left onto the King Side Tr. It passes through a beautiful forest with a high canopy that gives the woods an airy feel.

13. After 1.2k, you return to the main Bruce Tr., where you continue straight ahead following its white blazes.

14. When you come to a paved road (Kerns Rd.), turn left and follow it for 200m. Cross it and enter the City of Burlington's Kerncliff Park. Follow the main Bruce Tr. for about 100m and then continue walking toward the cliff. You leave the main Bruce Tr. and walk through to an unmarked but well-used city trail alongside a metal barrier.

15. Walk alongside this metal barrier, where there are great vistas, until it ends and joins the main Bruce Tr.

16. At this junction, veer right on the main Bruce Tr., with its white blazes, as it enters the forest.

17. After 500m you come to the Ian Reid Side Tr. He was the trail captain for the section of trail between King and Kerns roads for 40 years.

18. Turn right and follow the blue blazes of the Ian Reid Side Tr. It travels through a beautiful, deeply incised forest that is quite different from the flatter ones you've been travelling through. The trail includes a long uphill section, but it passes by enormous old-growth trees that were a delight for this dendrophiliac. Be careful to NOT pick up another side trail, which goes right after about 400m.

19. Upon reaching the end of the Ian Reid Side Tr., turn left and follow the white blazes of the main Bruce Tr. along a road-like path that runs atop a ridge. After about 100m, when the main Bruce Tr. veers left and dips down the ridge and back into the forest, you continue walking straight along the top of the ridge. This trail is part of the Burlington park system. It's nice to be

*A non-forested section of the Bruce Trail.* PHOTO BY MICHAEL DAVIS

out in the open for a bit. I stopped for lunch at 2 well-placed logs, where the main Bruce Tr. dips down the ridge. I had a great view and a fresh breeze.

20. This wide trail rejoins the main Bruce Tr. after about 400m. This time, rather than walking along the city trail with the metal barriers, follow the main Bruce Tr.

21. Pass by the King Side Tr. twice and the McNally Side Tr. once. Cross Mountain Brow Rd. and follow the white blazes along Flanders Dr.

22. Go left onto Redwood Pl. and continue past a set of gates at the end of the street. Just past here is the 128-year-old bitternut hickory.

23. The Upper Grindstone Side Tr. peels off to your right alongside a floodway, which is also on your right. You'll have to decide if it's worth walking up the hill and around this 1.1k loop. I figured that I needed to see what it had to offer. It's a nice piece of trail that takes you back down to the creek, and the hiking gods must have decided to reward my foray on your behalf because I came across a lovely white-tailed deer that hid behind some trees for a long time. In fact, I turned away before she did.

24. Upon completing the Upper Grindstone Side Tr., turn right and continue walking downhill. Cross busy Waterdown Rd. cautiously, and go down the stairs to the signpost where you began. Your car is parked on your right.

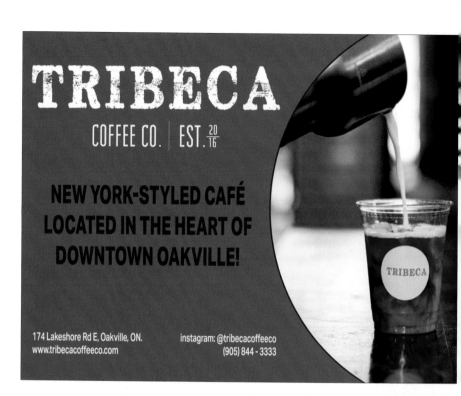

## Wild Birds Unlimited®
# save the song birds

**Visit wbu.com/save-the-song-birds**

# YOU CAN HELP

Food   Water   Cover   Places to Raise Young   Sustainable Practices

# Doing Your Best
# For the Birds

North American bird populations have declined by nearly 3 billion since the 1970s because of habitat loss, invasive species, climate change and pesticides. With a few simple actions, you can help make the world a better place for birds, wildlife and people, too.

**Here's a list of 7 Simple Actions you can take to help birds:**

1. Make Windows Safer
2. Keep Cats Indoors
3. Use Native Plants
4. Avoid Pesticides
5. Drink Shade-Grown Coffee
6. Use Less Plastic
7. Watch Birds, Share What You See

We bring people and nature together with excellence. • Your local backyard bird feeding specialists, we are a locally-owned business since 1994. • We proudly provide expert advice and personalized service so you can enjoy the birds in nature and in your own backyards. • Visit the store to see that we carry the freshest bird seed, the best feeders, baths, houses, feeder poles, optics & unique garden accents.

Nature Shop

**Wild Birds Unlimited**
3350 Fairview Street
Burlington ON - Ontario L7N3L5
905-634-7700
www.wbu.com/Burlington

BRUCE TRAIL  GRAND RIVER  NIAGARA ESCARPMENT

Something very unique happens when some of Canada's most beloved natural landscapes run right through a region's cities and towns. Getting out and exploring becomes second nature. When you're ready for a new breed of outdoor adventures that don't require a four-hour car ride to reach, Hamilton Halton Brant will be waiting for you.

**HAMILTON HALTON BRANT**
FIND YOUR WAY TO THE HEART OF ONTARIO

**FIND YOUR WAY TO THE HEART OF ONTARIO AND DISCOVER NATURE...UNEXPECTED.**
theheartofontario.com

ONTARIO
*Yours to discover*

Hamilton Halton Brant Regional Tourism Association is pleased to be a supporter of *Hamilton and Area Hikes: Loops & Lattes.*

Julia
Miss you

Miss my friend,
Cher.

Roseanne Ancher
Happy Hiking

Always warmly welcoming
Louise Stewart

♪ Happy Trails ♪♪
♥ Diane

In loving memory *Shirley E. White*
1950 ~ 2021
Your Wednesday Walkers

Will miss our adventures
Valerie

Dorothy Mazeau
You are in our hearts !

Mary Margaret Greyerbiehl
"Always in my heart."

SHIRLEY,
AN INSPIRATION
TO US ALL !
TORY XO

Thank you for
the many wonderful
hikes. Miss you.
Paula Bosciano

Cathy W.
" A FRIEND TO ALL ! "

Carol Blackmere
A best friend forever !

# The Loopy Ladies

*"Whatever our gift, we are called to give it
and to dance for the renewal of the world."*

Robin Wall Kimmerer from *Braiding Sweetgrass*

### NICOLA ROSS

Raised on Ontario's Niagara Escarpment, Nicola developed a keen sense of place at an early age. After pursuing her career in environmental studies and living away for nearly 20 years, she returned home. Once there, she engaged citizens in stewarding the area's precious countryside, often engaging her pen to achieve her goals. Some 2 decades later, Nicola is the award-winning author of 10 books, including the Loops & Lattes series. She has also published articles in *The Walrus,* the *Globe and Mail, Explore* magazine, *Mountain Life, The Bruce Trail* magazine and more. Between hikes, Nicola enjoys a great cup of coffee, preferably a dark roast served under a layer of foamy milk.
www.nicolaross.ca

### GILLIAN STEAD

Gill has been designing books most of her working life, covering a multitude of fascinating topics. Her subject matter ranges from Canada's boreal forest to West Coast cooking to Quebec folk art and the Costa Rican rainforest. She's designed books for such celebrated authors as James Raffin, Kevin Callan and Gary and Joanie McGuffin. Dark roast, Gill says, with splashes of milk & honey. gillianstead@rogers.com

### LORI-ANN LIVINGSTON

Lori-Ann Livingston is a writer and editor who first trained as a journalist, working for newspapers in the UK and southwestern Ontario. For 12 years, she worked in communications in the public sector. She also founded and ran an arts-based storytelling festival for 12 years. Lori-Ann has been published in *Broadview Magazine,* the *Globe and Mail* and *Alternatives Journal,* among others. Recently, she has been documenting the pandemic by walking, taking photos and writing a daily journal. Lori-Ann's java is flavoured, medium strength and served with cream. www.wordie.rocks

www.loopsandlattes.ca • hikeloopsandlattes@gmail.com • nicolaross.ca